For Rosemaria

all bless ? ?

Maur Harr

2001

Other books by CLAIRE HARRIS

She

CLAIRE HARRIS

GOOSE LANE

Book design by Julie Scriver.
Printed in Canada by AGMV Marquis.
10 9 8 7 6 5 4 3 2 1

Canadian Cataloguing in Publication Data

Harris, Claire, 1937-
She

Poems.
ISBN 0-86492-294-9

I. Title.

PS8565.A64825S54 2000   C811'.54   C00-900146-8
PR9199.3.H34588S54 2000

Published with the financial support of the Canada Council for the Arts, the Government of Canada through the Book Publishing Industry Development Program, and the New Brunswick Department of Economic Development, Tourism and Culture.

The author wishes to thank the Canada Council and the Alberta Foundation for the Arts for the grants which made this work possible, and Dr. Kenneth Ramchand, of the University of the West Indies, Trinidad, for the clue which led me out of the maze. Special thanks are owed to the National Documentation Centre, Roseau, Commonwealth of Dominica, West Indies, for their generous contribution of eleven pages of vocabulary lists, notes, and songs of the Carib peoples of the island, and especially to Ms A. Lewis, the Chief Librarian, who managed to get it all to me within a few hours, just before I left Grenada.
Versions of these pieces have appeared in *Descant* and *Kunapipi* (UK).

The Alberta
Foundation
for the Arts
COMMITTED TO THE DEVELOPMENT OF CULTURE AND THE ARTS

Alberta
COMMUNITY DEVELOPMENT

Goose Lane Editions
469 King Street
Fredericton, New Brunswick
CANADA E3B 1E5

I wish to thank John McDowell for editing this text
and for arranging that it arrive at the publishers
in suitable technological guise

AND

FOR HIS WILLINGNESS TO DANCE WITH LANGUAGE

She

Preface

If the phenomena of multiple personality seem wholly bizarre to the uninitiated, you can imagine how much more difficult it is to believe that a member of one's own very normal family is afflicted. The Three Faces of Eve stepping off the screen and into one's excessively ordinary life!

To our family, my sister, Penelope-Marie, was the artistic, dramatic, literary one. Even before she left school, and certainly while at university, Penny often wrote ten — or fifteen — page letters in a highly literary mixture of poetry and prose. Little scenes would arrive as if life were a play, an entertainment laid on by the world for her amusement. Sometimes those plays were about us. It amazed — perhaps, more honestly, annoyed — us when she began to publish. Penny wasn't discreet, and was much given to what we viewed as extravagant exaggeration.

With the vision of hindsight, I think she may have been a difficult child. But I can say only that she seemed to enjoy her own company and seemed to me, ten years younger, to do exactly as she wished. Perhaps she read far too much; we thought this accounted for her sometimes very English turns of speech. An odd child. She never grew out of any of this or out of her wild, continually changing enthusiasms. In the Caribbean, we considered her behaviour a moral problem. She was "some-timish": socially unpredictable, eminently selfish. She was also an exhibitionist: one never knew what "costume" she would turn up in, what language she would speak. If she would speak. But no one ever thought of her as ill. Of course, I had never been told about Thena.

In the last few months, I was deluged with letters from Penny; there was mail everyday, often several envelopes, or faxes. I have included almost all of these letters in this collection, omitting only the shortest notes, one-liners, poems, "scenes," newspaper clippings. Her letters appear here in the order in which they were received.

Jasmine-Marie Lancet Maine
2000

Penny Performs

dear jasmine

beyond the harvest of faces winnowed in bathroom mirrors
this past week bedraggled a cat caught in rainstorm
today's khaki sky sprawls pungent over calgary
twists the traffic's white hum to grind and jar greases
flyovers tags the hazed purse-lipped iron bridges
with ragged promise the river refuses this nicotine
light retires from reflection into skin
which here and there creases
where trout slide by
or winged water things trembling feast
our north bank's modest villages time's cul-de-sacs
touched with the gentle ungentle huddle under
wait a drunken boot in the trees' flattened tops
silent jays black question marks flown this tight
bed where steel gleams from caring smiles while seeming far
our glasshenge pride and rue altars hushed sanctuaries
grey-suited nuns monks pin-striped acolytes stranger
ceremonies where desire's measured counted out
in highest crannies bald raptors nest wild
glut swoop glide remember don't you
how beyond law the buskers seductive private music
like a shower in desert wastes
how energy shapes power dims hallways byways hush
money gossip and yet beyond that musty bruising sky
the spirits of those denied roof huts raise
lodge poles forage hunt sound and are

sounded in a clear perpetual blue

well why not?
who absorbs only
what you call
"the dark"?
miss
under
standing

who playing at gardens
ignores the devil
knitting hedges?

here
there is
this

jahmin
after all
my truth searches the blank spaces
yours the web and tangle of your life
consider me
if at all
an enabler
this the fixer or stop bath

meanwhile despite narrow room high window absence of silence scent
that shape-shifts nightmare in(re)jection's sharp pinch careful airs nagging
a constant swallow of pills and saccharin soothing today eyes sealed as
if the earth had not opened its arms i limbo
in the green-stippling
in poplars

in net of bird cries
                    hatched wind
          under my lids   i curve i bend
     the blue rinsed Bow   i shimmy
       the circling gulls   in branching richness of cedars
         small boys hoot   among mango leaves and sibilance
   the blue crowned motmot   i roll to the tamboo bamboo
      even so   i am that woman clenched around deep darkness
         my soles cling to crabgrass my toes treading
              dark water i heel into worm casts
          the fruitful invisible life's faint signals
                    squashed

          . . . is groan yuh groaning?
                    is how you ent . . .

               yet how is it
     i write to you of painful whirling falls momentary
absence blankness   you write back
                    "silence is not such a bad thing"?
          an exile i think of "home" sky/earth/wind-forested hills
hungry greens circling blues reds orange   tangled valley

               . . . amusing really the way She clings
                 to the glamour of "exile"
                    have you lot noted . . .

starred verges tumbling towards
our road its bright roofs its light pregnant curtains
its old men their lancing eyes hard-scabbed dry-wrinkled
hands the careful individual doors entrances
into an old formality and
                    secret

and i think "safe"
think "net" though knowing
today mcdonald's cuckoo-ed into those clefts and
CNN nests even as i dream
our green life-haunted tropical womb
needing to i think nosy but caring
an essential warmth sometimes easy forgiveness
always soft airs and breezes

. . . sheesh — "saft air an' breeze"
is sun like bull pistle an' days ha' no wind . . .

and now my sister
writes "you should rejoice at your gift
for escaping the world"!
oh damn . . . oh oh shhh
you can't believe the sudden headaches
my mountainous head rock-cleft
earth whirling past
mouth stuffed
melancholy and aspirin

. . . lissen gurl is dead She a'most dead
dis not time fuh mamaguy
we ent come to yuh fuh backchat nor
for squeeze eider   dis true-true stuff scratch
come scary is rise from yuh ease an' ge wit' it   time
yuh know wha doctah here cyan figure mus' be in yuh head . . .

. . . say god say rod staff
say good night to jassy . . .

. . . well sisters of brave mettle
we have lifted the moon out of her sphere . . .

. . . pen-e-lope yuh worse dan She you know dat . . .
    ah the interrupti
now do we not shak 'n' spear the moments
of this our victory

. . . steups! victory! is look at my crosses now . . .

ms lancet wait my moment please
            here pale butterflies and yellow
                            swooping far sky

            ichthyornis
        spirit wheels laughing

penelope, yuh done finish? ah could talk?
dear mAri!
is a hospital. ah ent lyin here while youso fool aroun typin book. ah
goin out. now. aftah ah get some clothes orn. allyuh forget life swifter
dan a tanager, fade faster dan a four o'clock. is how anybody could
design stuff like dis fuh adult? it come straight from some nursary. yuh
know wha dese shiftso say? "yuh come in mi horspital you is chile.
doan be tinkin yuh know wha you feel, even how yuh feel it. Doc pa an
ma nurse goin decide." gawd! buh dis body feel like drought, yes. ah
move, it crack. an dis floor well arctic! Eh Eh! is so? allyou realize it ent
ha' nutten in dis lockah? dey stealway we clothes! dey bettah lemme
outa here! Lemme OOOUT . . .
    mAri, for God sake, girl, be quiet! please to let She sleep. you want
we be stuck in this hospital for ever?
    ms lancet, is me yuh blamin? ent is allyou de nurse nearly ketch?

you can't see they think She writing away her problem?

the more She take themso serious, do what they want, the quieter we is, is quicker we getting out.

ms lancet yuh cyan pay dese people no mind; yuh gotta stop playin dey game by dey rule. yuh ge' we in enough trouble, de more all youso type is longa we stay here.

we could be famous! a case in the lancet. by the lancets. disputes. talk shows. perhaps there'll be a film! i'll get . . .

penelope go sleep. yuh ent ha' sense enough to know is so deyso want stifle we. bad enough is yuh call ambulance.

mAri, did you really expect She to have a child alone at home? it couldn't be done. tell her ms lancet. can you imagine a home-hysterical-birth? after that pregnancy? we couldn't help, you know, at least i couldn't, i'm not into pain.

penelope both you an mAri know full well, and is not pleased i pleased to say this, it ain't necessarily false pregnancy eh!

knew it! i've always had hopes for that sea green outfit. it would be perfect for a court app . . .

gurl, it ent ha' nutten yuh ent need prop for?

(moan/deep sigh/gosh!/sigh)

Props! Are you writing a play, Penny? My gosh, you've done a lot! A bit too much shouting in here, of course, people are trying to rest. But with all the different voices, it sounds exciting. Why aren't you in bed? Can't you sleep?

Not really, nurse.

You need your rest, I'll straighten these sheets. Doctor said you were to have these. Are you typing everything I say?

All grist for the mill. I've had enough pills; they'll make me woozy. What I actually have is a headache!

Penny, I know you don't like pills, but sleep will help, really. More water? Good! You're a tough lady, we're all so proud of how well you're doing.

In another couple of days you'll be out of here. Sleep well. I'll turn off your light.

No! Don't do that, I'll turn it off myself. In a minute. Thanks!

Not too long now! I'll look in later.

Drugs! Drugs! drugssssdru . . .

tough lady! giggle gigglegigglegiggle . . .
lord spare us, allyou better stop with the giggling or
somebody going come back in here, yes.
okay, ms lancet, but you've got to admit . . .
shush!

jahmin

i am gone into winter
and hope
alone

in some not-here not-here not . . .

is so all men go, jass, de rest is silence. oh Gawd! allyuh
ent hear me! pen-e-lope like a disease.   jass gurl, is sleep
She gorn to sleep!

love to allyou dere!

mAri
for penny

Penny Performs

dear jassy

i'm back home, as you see. i wrote this for her. before they told me, of course. would you mind a second-hand poem for Cyril Lionel Robert? perhaps he would enjoy it. you musn't worry; i'll be all right soon. my strength's coming back already. tell the aunts i'm following all the advice down to the warm coconut oil. you might want to change the name in this. i couldn't.

love

penny

CHARLA'S TOWER POWER

Sixteen Charlas in the gloom such a small small room
hear honk! honk!
            geese in a wild
quicksilver sky
Charlas in fear there's the broom AND the bear
hover in their doom
hushhh! soft on the stair a slither and snarboom
oh quick! Charlas try a wild wilder dare
you two get this chair that chair pile them here
twelve Charlas must shear and share their hair
while this Charla listens where

wild honking

                              geese

quicksilver sky

Now fourteen knit a snare Charlas in a square swift!
no time to sneer! we can't spare fingers or hair
you others pile sofa table book just here
before the door
                      ere the bear his teeth
                          gleaming bare
        or the broom slithers near and nearer

            while quicksilver wild
                                    in honk
                  a geese-sky

Quick, Charlas! hurry no flurry or scurry
                          climb
                           on
                          this
                          sill
                          feet
                           to
                       shoulder
                         form
                       a tower

                      Charla
                   at the top!
                 fling the snare!

NOW! GO ON! T H E R E!
with the geese on a wing and a prayer
away from the bear from broom-slither on the stair
from this crazy woman's stare

to sky

geese

honk

in a wild

wild

quick

silver

THE END

PS   would that we were all so lucky!

Penny Peforms

dear jahmin

i am not a shadow
or even a drift
from an other time

i am fiction

so who writes me?

love

penny

mAri Performs

dear jass

dis is jes
to say
i fin' dis
in de out tray
an now sen'in
it to yuh

so cole
so mad an' baaad
like a stone trown
                        enjoyin
                          it own arc
                            it shatterin
                        contract
                  wid glass
it brazen splintery
lannin

jes banal
to tink us aberashun
wha dere
to heal
in we variousness?
we who ent
flourish
ent metaphor

dis is jes'
to say
we is no
fragment so
we is we own
undah long
divishun
undah multiplicashun

sepahrate
as perfic' as
each floret
of de oleander
each keel
of hangin heliconia
as necessary
in we beautee
as necessary
as breat'

we so strange
we so entiah
is simple as honey
still fuh tea
we bloom
we strengt'
startle
yeah
leh we spit
on dis ordinary
doh we make it
togedder
yeah   us so spit

on integrashun
it swallow-up an'
buryin
leh we be
we own constellashun
a whole distric'
in orbit

is why we so
got to consent
bowin an'
kowtowin
to oblivion?

love

mAri

Penny Performs

The Sun Stone's Revenge

In the mirrored wall she looked thinner, significantly so, in spite of her stomach. Paler too. The golden yellow underlying her dark brown skin had given way to grey. Her hair had grown. Tight, springy new growth coiled close to her scalp. The straightened, brittle length tucked into shaggy dull wisps behind her ears.

old aunties shelling peas on the verandah pale faces lofted from curved backs rising out of shadow to say hair grows after you're dead and your nails memory of hard brushes

She stared at the bag. It was very light. An airline bag from the sixties. The navy nylon with red trim and BWIA written on it seemed vaguely familiar. She carried it over her right shoulder and the bag swung every time she moved because there was nothing in it except a strange burnt-apricot tie-dyed African gown and an empty wallet. She had tried to point out that the gown could not be hers. Really. The new student nurse had shushed her, looking around first as if to check, then insisted. She was good at conspiracy. Had roused herself sufficiently to make no further objections. To assist. That was how she'd also acquired the wallet. Not hers either. Well, it was empty now. There had been four quarters, a dime, a nickel, seven pennies, a toonie and two loonies. There was also a business card. She, or the nurse, had given the card to the cabbie at the hospital. When he drew up at the apartment building, turned to her blank stare and insisted, "This is it, lady, six dollars," she had simply handed him the wallet. Disgusted, he had counted every coin aloud, stared at her, shook his head, then got out of the car to help her up the stairs to a slate grey lobby. The doors were locked against her. "Buzz the manager, lady!" A contemptuous pity. She'd complied helplessly. He'd waited, hands smug in the pockets of his shabby ski jacket, leaning against the wall to examine tight plantations of plastic rubber trees boxed into a corner opposite the newspapers. "Think these are real? I never can tell."

He was making conversation. She knew that.

"They're dead," she'd replied. An effort.

At last, the manager. He seemed to know her. "Oh, Miss Lancet, you're back." In the mirror she was wearing cords, sneakers without socks, a huge baggy fisherman's knit sweater. None of it looked familiar. The sleeves someone had pushed up her lower arms had begun to slide down towards her wrists.

"Had a good holiday? Great weather for it! It's been raining here since you left."

Nothing.

There was a notice in the elevator. *The water will be turned off July 14, from 9 am to 4 pm to allow the city to work on the mains* . . . He saw her staring at it and said, "I've got to remind the wife to fill some jugs."

She supposed he was reminding her. "I was learning how to golf." Her voice was rusty.

He smiled. "Really, where did you go?"

She leaned against the back of the elevator, felt her bag bump against her stomach. She saw . . . Sandy, that was his name; she saw his smile slip from his face, twist into dismay, blanket itself in blindness. Then she heard the harsh choking sounds, felt her chest tighten, her shoulders heave, looked down at the warm plop of tears falling onto the hand clasped across her stomach. Her crying stopped as suddenly as it had begun, and she was there staring at the notice while the slowest elevator in Calgary moved silently to the tenth floor.

"Are you sure you're all right?" He was standing in the entrance of apartment 911. The door was open. She supposed she should go in. She turned in the tiny square hall. He was still there. It was bad manners to bang the world shut. She spoke hurriedly, loudly, to catch the half of his face still visible as the door swung to. "Thanks! Fine! Fine!"

Still carrying the bag, she walked into a rich narrow room walled with east light, sat down on a long sofa. Bereft. She looked around at the empty room; she had stumbled into silence. She sat up to listen and knew it was worse than that. She had been silenced. Her breathing too slow, too faint to disturb air. Alone beyond belief. She couldn't live in this. She began to bawl. Heard herself calling out Charla Lancet . . . Charla Angela . . . Charla Angela Lancet . . . Charla . . . Ange . . . No answer. Nothing in the angles of the room. There drifted across her mind a memory of green balconies, of having searched . . . She tried once again, CharlaAnge . . . Her voice a plea, a whisper . . . Charla?

She was pounding on cushions, sweeping books off the coffee table, hurling red, yellow Venetian bits against the far walls. She was howling. It was not enough. She tore her clothes off and rolled around on the floor. Grabbing a table loaded with parcels, mail, a mask, she dragged herself upright. A crash. Something against her shins. She rummaged in kitchen drawers until she found shears and, shrieking, attacked first her hair, then the discarded sweater. It was not enough. When the blade plunged into her thigh there was no feeling, just blood welling up. Harsh guttural noises hung about her head. She plunged the blade in. In again in again inagain inagain inininin. Then turned to the other thigh. The wells flamed. It was not enough. Again and again. Oh God! OH and Oh and OH! A terrible burning where the gashes puckered, tried to seal themselves. Then she stopped. Stopped and collapsed shuddering, her back against a low book case, slashed thighs staining the white carpet. A spreading and pooling without interest.

"Who would have thought the old man to have so much blood in him. . ." Her school girl voice rising to a shriek, sparking. She waited for the response. For the North Sea "Overdramatizing as usual" to clip across the giggling colonial silence. It didn't come. After a while she realized it wouldn't. Her thighs hurt like hell. She had to staunch the blood. She crawled across the floor to where bits of cream woollen sweater lay unravelling. Held strips to her thighs, held other strips and others. Then she made a species of bandage from torn bra and ripped panties and tied her self together.

It was enough. For what?

She was in the shower weeping where water nibbled then ate at her thighs, grasping the flesh, biting her lips as she poured on Dettol and applied Elastoplast. Then she was standing in front of a mirror trying to plait jagged lengths of hair into cornrows. Afterwards she washed her face again, used the clear acrylic brush in the yellow tooth mug, put on the crisp green cotton nightgown she found hanging behind the bathroom door. Then she had to turn down the radio, check the alarm, fold the bedspread halfway down, switch off the main lights, pull the bedroom door shut. She wondered at the Yale lock before turning it, testing. There was a glass on the bedside table. It had to be filled. Water? Milk? Whiskey? The woman who had chosen those red and tan shower curtains, the storm cloud walls and the pale ceiling would have whiskey. She wouldn't.

When she came back into the room, an inch of lukewarm water

shaking in her grasp, she found herself hesitating, shrinking from the city flinging itself against the glass wall. There were vertical blinds hidden behind side drapes. But the stuff was heavy and dusty, useless triple folds unmoving. She couldn't work the blinds either. She was too tired. Climbing clumsily, heavily into bed, she reached for the sheet to pull it over her head, then turned on her side, making a space for her tummy. She somehow over-rotated, at least that's what it felt like, and she was lying on a gashed thigh. She cried out with the pain of it, and shifted herself more carefully. It hurt like hell. She reached out blindly in the dark and her fingers closed on an aspirin bottle. She took four, lay waiting in faintly scented silence and in the light from the window.

It was enough. For what?

Tired . . . beyond belief.

When she closed her eyes, an incredible image: a monstrous tangle of vines snaking on a mustard background. She sat up instantly. Her mouth was dry, her heart pounding. She looked around wildly. Then, recognizing the room, she relaxed. She had forgotten. No sleep. She mustn't let herself fall asleep . . .

She was pushing a huge stomach through a psychedelic forest. The earth was a cool dark chocolate colour, giving off the smell of fresh rain, she was describing what she saw and the hill in front of her. They wanted her to climb the hill. A man was making warm encouraging noises. He was black. She knew that as she knew the doctor was white. It was their voices. She couldn't turn around or look at them. It would spoil the experiment. The leaves were a forest of exclamations shimmering all along the branches and so dense that it was impossible to see the sky. She moved through a bright gloom toward the road at the top of the hill. It was steep and she was unusually clumsy. Several times she had to put her fingers down to the ground to prevent the stomach from pulling her over. When she wanted to turn back they wouldn't let her. It would spoil the experiment. She was getting more and more tired. She had promised. She would have to make it up the slope to tell them what was there. She could hear water gurgling over stones; there was a river fairly close by. Something cool brushed against her cheek and she looked up to see a brilliant creamy-white bladderwort dangling beside the cocoa ripening in the branches. She knew where she was now. The plantation behind the house. She would scramble up the last bit; it would be hot, and the tar would be soft under her heels, though mango trees, sapodillas arched green over the road. Beyond the bend she would see the mosque, and not very much further on the opposite side the temple with the flags fading red and pink and perhaps white. There would be a breeze. Not sure about the white. She took another step forward and heard the warning rattle. Snake. She stopped dead. Go on. Go on. The man was saying Go on. No. She said No. Go on, you must; you'll spoil everything. She remembered then she was in a wheelchair in a hospital. If she opened her eyes it would stop. They couldn't make her. Don't someone said. But she opened her eyes and said No very calmly. As if she were someone who usually said yes or no and meant it . . .

She woke as if from a jostling of voices. Her mind terrifyingly clear. She sat a long while, soft city light hugging her knees. Then she turned to look at her crisp outline in the mirrored doors. Right! She got out of bed, found white jeans, a white t-shirt, white sneakers, heavy leather gloves, a scarf. It took her fifteen minutes to find the weapon. She'd bought it in a market in the Sahel because it reminded her of home, childhood, Arouca. Things that had seemed sweetly worth remembering at the time. In the end she had to dump everything from the bottom drawer of The Greats' old sea-chest.

the airy dimness of old tropical houses.
"why it is she think she got to take everything new there? is don't remember you don't want to remember your family or what?"
"is too stubborn she stubborn! this have history!"
they'd talked around her as if she weren't there. she'd done what she always did under such circumstances. whistled tunelessly under her breath. in the end the trunk had migrated with her and with it the skills she hadn't remembered she had.

She brought herself back with an effort. There it was, packaged with stones in a leather bag. She emptied the whole lot into a fanny pack. Belted it on. Her hands were calm, sure. She had plenty of time. She knelt awkwardly on the floor, began to examine each skirt, shawl, each nightgown, its crocheted lace or cross-stitching. It took a while before she could move on to the tiny garments. She'd embroidered them herself according to custom. Sheets and soft fleecy blankets, bought ready-made but edged with her own crocheted lace. There was the robe they had been christened in. She and all her brothers. She held each garment, each piece or length of fabric against the light, rather as a relative might. Some fond aunt after a sudden death, smoothing and folding carefully into the original creases, replacing the envelopes of tissue paper, before laying it back into the drawer. When the kente cloth, the handwoven black and white place mats, the ivory paper knife, the joke paper napkins, the wooden clappers which once called Malian women to prayer, the copper carnival tiles, the tie-dyed table cloth with its sets of contrasting and matching napkins had all been put back, she had to jiggle the drawer gently to get it to slide into its grooves.

In the top shelf of the trunk she found a box, empty in spite of small pieces of cloth. Strangely, one shelf in her bookcase had been turned into a Yoruba shrine. Fertility, birth, gladness. Shrugging, a trifle uneasy, she walked down the dark hall, found the brandy glass of matchbooks, a large plate, milk, honey, olive oil, rum. Her hand closed around these things sure and knowing. In the bedroom, she prayed. Kneeling, bowing, promising, thanking. Then she burnt the offerings of food she had placed there before going to the hospital, poured her libation on the carpet. Dissatisfied with this distance from truth, she stepped out onto the balcony and high on the bluff over her electric city, poured another libation onto northern earth. Afterwards she dismantled the shrine, kissing the swollen breasts, belly, the elegant geometry of the goddess, the sweet curves and roundness that were the daughter, before wrapping each piece into its original cloth and placing it in the box. Then she found the little brass key and locked it all away.

At two a.m. she let herself out of the apartment. Walked into the comfortable shadows. She tried to force herself not to limp. Then remembered she'd left the hospital apparently whole. A limp was a great disguise. But in the eight blocks to the hospital she met no one. There were no cars waiting at the lights on Memorial. When she emerged from Meredith to cross Edmonton Trail, she was exposed to a light cool breeze from the river. It was strangely liberating to be alone in the night, Bridgeland tucked in and dreaming. From Centre Avenue hill she looked down to where Calgary glimmered jagged white, yellow, green and red, all elongated in the Bow waters. A car slid to a racing stop, moved on before the light changed. She watched as if from some far world. Then she came down to the hospital. It waited islanded on its dim plain of concrete bordered by black clumps of pine and broken rows of what she knew were cherry trees. She stood for a moment sloshing around in an ocean of revulsion. The humming in her head throbbed into sound; should have blown it all to a mess of stone, twisted steel. Mushroom cloud blossoming brown and sharply lit within.

She crossed the tungsten-yellow tarmac, flung an aching leg over railings, into the trees. Then she walked calmly across the dimly lighted car park. About two dozen cars were scattered between the fluorescent yellow lines of this lot, and she half turned sideways to slip between them. When she gained the sidewalk, she walked coolly to the side door, opened it and stepped into the familiar dim machine hum of the Old Building. The corridor led to the main hall. At right angles there was another. It led to offices. Doctors. Dr. Gangston's office was at the far corner of this building. His window looking out on the lawn at the back of the hospital. Near his office there were stairs going down to the basement. Housekeeping. Down there she would find the white coat she needed.

Pipes. Clanging. Whirring. Machines at labour as she had been. Voices. Boiled linen smell seeping from under the closed double doors that confronted her. As long as they didn't open. She was standing in an anteroom: chutes, wheeled bins shaped like giant spades. Soiled sheets, patient gowns, bins that smelled of blood, sickness. At the far end, white coats. She had to stand on tiptoe to pull several out before she found one that fit and had merely been worn. After transferring gloves from the pocket of a coat with yellow stains, she slipped the green hunting jacket off, hung it with the other coats on the far wall.

She saw the Filipina nurse before she saw her. So she was ready with a smile and "How's it going?"

The other barely lifted her head. "I'm dead."

She smiled sympathy and, when the nurse turned away down the corridor, went on into the hall, up the elevator to the first floor. The night watchman was not on his desk. Bloody stupid! Anyone could come in. Murder the patients in their beds. Those halls had been full of watchmen the one time she'd tried to leave. She took the elevator to the fourth floor, stepped out into the foot clinic. There was, of course, no one at the reception desk. The lights low and mournful. Down in the same elevator and back into the main hall again. She stumbled, pushed back the clanging door. The watchman was back. He looked up, called out, "You okay?" as if he meant it. She made a pantomime of rubbing her side and elbow. She grinned ruefully, took the pack of cigarettes out of her bag and lit one as she passed him.

"Hey there! Wait, can't you!"

She waved nonchalantly at him over her shoulder.

Once outside she sat on a cold concrete bench against the wall. She would have to smoke. Three years as a non-smoker. Something else Gangston owed her. Her body rose to meet the exhilarating tang and scratch, the furl of smoke in her throat, the scent, the ritual. She inhaled deeply. Hooked again. But there was no point in stopping now. Every cloud has a silver etc . . . etc. She seemed to wait there forever, establishing character, she thought, bona fides. You are a nurse on her break. You've been working nine hours, you have three Klein hours left. Take every last second of your fifteen minutes.

The watchman, his body slumped on blue cotton forearms, was deep in *Popular Mechanics*. She walked briskly through the doors, down the hall to the elevators, pressed the button for the eighth floor, slipped out again, and walked briskly up the short hall on her left. The watchman's nose was still buried in his magazine. She slid through the inner door and out through the fire doors to the parking lot. She had been kept on the third floor in the East Wing. She counted the windows, then found a car at the right distance and braced herself. The slingshot felt clean, easy in her hand. She was the stone, the wide sharp-edged one. The rubber drew back. She was catapulted from the sling. Felt the small resistance of glass. Heard its tinkle and crash. The sling smoked twice again. Sticking as close to the building as possible, she ran back around to the West Wing. When the glass collapsed in Gangston's window, shards scattering like spears, she pulled on black winter gloves over the rubber ones she'd found. Sudden paralysis grabbed her. Slow glass tinkled. Eyes closed.

> . . . steups! is why She doan lif' de windoh!
> ain't i tell allyou, do it yourself? what if She get ketch?
> chile! pull yuhself together! eh eh! hurry up! . . .

Like a tap-tapping to attention. Chac-chac held to the ear. Startled, she flung one damaged thigh over, jumped through, brought the frame down again. She stepped carefully past the mess on the floor, trying not to hurry in spite of the wailing of police sirens. There was a short hall leading to the office bathroom where she had reason to know there was a toilet, wash basin and narrow metal locker. She slid quickly into the locker and coiled into fetal position, pressing as far back as possible. She left the door very slightly ajar. She didn't think anyone would look. Luckily it hadn't rained for weeks. She remembered the unchanging square of taunting blue sky in her hospital room. Her watch glowed three o'clock. She heard the footsteps. Cops calling to each other. Someone found the stone. Someone else shone a light into the room. Its narrow beam lingered on floor and ceiling. Footsteps, a breathy voice. Someone threw a switch. She had stopped breathing long ago. Forever. Finally the lights went out. She heard the office door shut. After a while, hammering at the window. Uncoiled, she sat with her back to the locker. Slipped into reverie . . . perhaps he'd thought she'd never remember. The bab . . . she began to tremble. She must not think of that. Not yet. But the pills, the tears, the questions, the needles, the tapes, the vomiting, the too-thorough physicals, the student doctors, the constant examinations, the student doctors, the needles, the notebooks. The bilious room. She counted to a hundred . . .

Really a urine-coloured room. She was lying on her back in a hospital bed. Her stomach rose like a mountain. After her late-night shot, temperature, blood pressure, she climbed out of bed and went to the window. This wasn't easy. There was a building opposite. In its window high-fashion models posed. She knew they posed for her. None of this was possible. She knew it. All pictures. Film? Only they looked so real. She wanted to wave at those beautiful black women. They were black. Lacquered, of course, but still . . . she waved and smiled. They didn't move. The baby kicked and kicked again as she turned back toward the bed. She climbed into bed slowly. When she woke, the great mound was gone. Her stomach a little distended but clearly empty. She had got up, crying out, calling for a nurse. They had strapped her to the bed. They said "No." No? "NO!" Sometimes they said, "So sorry, no." No. She soon saw that if she continued to say "Yes," if she insisted, she would never be allowed to leave. What would happen to Charla Ange then? More needles, more notebooks. It was confusing, tiring. Trying to decide all the time what was real what wasn't. What it was safe to say what wasn't. And time seemed to drift past her. There was another woman in the hospital room. She turned, saw her watching her.

"Did you see?" she asked, straining against the straps, gesturing to her stomach. "No," the woman said and turned over on her side, facing the wall. She sounded embarrassed.

One morning she woke, the cotton wool in her head thinning. She knew they had made the woman say that. She began to cheek her pills. She lay back in the hospital bed, trying to think. She needed help. She'd signed . . . a vague memory of forms. It was a long while later. Days perhaps. The singing had awakened her. There was another window in the room. This one was right in front of her bed. A folk choir in West Indian costume! How could they bring those people in here? She was sick. Her hair wasn't done. This was going too far. She probably worked with some of those people. She rushed out of bed and into the long dim corridor. Then she remembered. She was barefoot. Naked under a blue gown open at the back. She came back into the room. Walked over to the foot of the other woman's bed. "Look," she said, "will you help me?"

"I'll do what I can. But I have to be careful." The woman was whispering. "They're operating on me tomorrow. Nobody, nobody deserves to be treated like that . . ."

There was nothing one could do about drugs injected.

She was searching the long corridors of the General Hospital. She was looking for something in rooms and hall closets, on trays, in baskets, in the stairwells. She began to think what she sought must be on another floor. She'd searched, kept searching everywhere. The same places again and again. She was going through the bathrooms one by one, avoiding the knowing mirrors. She was walking into rooms, their sleeping or startled faces on the pillows. Searching. When the phone rang . . .

She jerked awake. It was 4:10 a.m. The phone in the office continued to ring. She had an hour and a half. She waited impatiently in the locker for it to stop. Then waited again. After a few minutes, she entered the room. The blinds had been pulled down. She listened at the door, the window. Nothing. She found the tapes easily. Well, not *the* tapes, just tapes. She didn't intend to check. The tape recorder was on a shelf. She began to erase. She found notebooks that went into coat pockets, fanny pack. The disks were nowhere to be found. The filing cabinet. She broke it open. Easy. Steph, the building manager at work, had taught her when she lost her keys that third time. There were about fifty disks. A small panic before she remembered the magnet in the back pocket of her white jeans. By six she was finished. Disks erased. Memory emptied. Notebooks, his diary in the pockets of the white coat. Tapes clean. She did not touch the files. His research was not in them, only his victims.

She put everything back neatly on the shelves, as she had found them. Remembered to close the filing cabinet, cover the expensive computer. He had been about forty-five. Not had been, was. For a few weeks at least, nobody would die here. She hoped he wasn't the sort who kept copies of disks at home.

She ditched the coat and rubber gloves in the laundry room, collected her jacket and left with the night shift, hurrying. Her face, like theirs, already turned towards the other life and home. Her white jeans, white t-shirt, sneakers, a little more dusty than theirs. No one seemed to notice. Everything must go into the garbage. The new hunting jacket in the city container behind the Latvian Church. The slingshot in the Bow. She had to hurry. The city collected before seven.

She had never realized how fresh and sweet such early morning air could seem or how strong she was. She whistled her way home tunelessly.

and now
how lightly
she goes on trails
where stones harrow her steps
where the debris of fables chittering
from margins are poisonous
lightly
where few have passed before
twisted moss
in abominations still
she goes lightly
and lightly she
lightly goes
where rocks grin
and the sky's white tongue embalms
through clefts into valleys
goes she deeper
where the will grows bottomless
and safety flees with fear
deeper
though the Bow guiding her
freezes into spring
though she goes where the heart
strains at the leash
and breath slows to the strum of despair
she goes lightly
so lightly she
brittle feet chipped
in ground winds
air churning with the thrum of wings
lightly
furiously
she dances on rims

Penny Performs

dear jahmin

now morning kneels down in the dust
          where the woman drifts empty rooms ghost
listening
          the child's cry

                         absence she learns is not a void

day running after day running
without &
with out

                         or interruption
such days
               a swift procession
          funerals
     dry footsteps through the ruins
               a lengthening dante

i am without ground

                              still the apartment holds
this voice an answering machine informs a world vanishing
soft dust sifting the air
                    She "is not available"
                         and She isn't
          eventually i hush the phone

notes irrelevant moments
newspapers all stacking themselves
on the kitchen table
                    cease rustling   their/our searching passage

. . . where once we swam warm salt water pools of promise
where once our laughter charmed rocky peaks into forest
        flaring winged colour
                              each moment budding
        bloomed soft sweets or sharp of thyme vanilla lime
once hyacinth frangipani swayed and lingered in our rooms . . .

        . . . sigh sigh cough cough . . . upstairs and downstairs
and in my lady's chamber . . . giggle giggle gigglegigglegiggle . . .

        now everywhere mirrors
        narrowing passages
                                              and such images
now i query each hour of confinement
        each quarter each minute
                              birthing

. . . and She is a carpenter constructing shelter
                planing each board matching grain
                        mallet sure on each wooden peg . . .

. . . actually is more a hawk circlin'
                deadly in she plummet toward . . .

                                  baby girl

my Charla

stay against extinction

perhaps

like this piecing out the self

. . . sole meaning . . .

. . . meaning my foot! is right here allyou got real problems. read too much understanding nothing. book ain't world, allyou fall gyrating through the self. is modern trap. God help She! extinction! once you made you made it ain't have no void after that. by the way i am marie lancet. who are you? we hear you all the time but you don't identify yourself. hello? hello?

zzzzzzzzzzzzzzzzzzzzzzzzzzzzzzzz

but is why you don't answer? we need to talk, man, is . . .

. . . silence plucked like a berry . . .

at least, please tell us about the child there with you

zzzzzzzzzzzzzzzzzzzzzzzzzzzzzzzzzzzzzzz

okay then, think about it, please. is important. rie?

it ent me, ms lancet

i know that child, but we-all need to think about what to do. all allyou better pray, yes. Lord! is so penny in pieces, less and less She returning to Sheself. is like She loss in all them mirror doors round the house. an' is not as if anybody here like dem things, is always mirror mirror on the wall an' something shadowy floating. is not like you could even see your face clear. steups! anyway what i coming to understand, nowadays it ain't enough for woman to live, to grow in she soul. you got to produce something. is why She fix on baby. and is why She busy writing everything every thing down. i just wait till she gorn then i burn them in the sink. who want people knowing this foolishness? importance. is a disease we ketch, this marking the world. you life as graffiti.

now for She it no longer have fullness of moment. only product. jasmine girl, your sister like She come factory. or worse, some machine blind to everything but motion. She fraid to sit still, to think. She fraid to dream. She fraid even sleep. all day She reading from book to book, pause for a drink, eat book in hand what somebody cook. book become drug. i suppose you can't blame She for that.

in life everything everything what ever happen hide inside you, crouch like a thief to take all what you have from you. every mistake, every hurt and shame, every foul laugh, even every joy, success, love, good thing way back to the womb. human being well complicated. lucky for most people like you, jasmine, all that stuff tie down real strong tie down with steel. in your sister only thin rope to fray. now most everything floating loose, bobbing about inside She, knocking into each other coming up for air. and the hurt so strong. but is what lying in mud is what down there feeding what give real trouble. is so it come She walking 'bout under the rockies, but She don't see, can't see anything, can't even feel . . .

. . . how they sit there
androgynous
mountain ranges embroidered
against sky knotted deep in earth's core . . .

. . . no no
all what She see
is avalanche
seasons in
relentless tumbling   snow
green
harvest moons
granite
spring only a sliver bloom
belayed summer and
winter's white womb

you think such slow revolutions
anyone at all
anyone bound to know
in the bone

is a circling a making whole
                 but not at all at all

no

                                   for She part
                   is break change scatter
            separate from Sheself
                      no call to see the world
              come only a glass bubble
                         better yet a stage
                                 scenery athwart
            is so trouble start
            now trucks fly trains sail off their tracks
                    trees wave their roots
                 stones quack . . .

                 . . . jass gurl, rie here,
              She life lopsided
                      tink of a ole lady bend
                             double an limpin
                             outa noonday sun
                             is so She is

                             under de hood dem eyes
                      frantic wit' life
                             an' tenacious knowin . . .

       . . . is talk She talk like She gorn. buh even in de midnight pane
             yuh see in dose eyes reflec' back at yuh . . .

             time-caught between

i thin lose dimension
                              even the Bow
                    lets me down
                                        into
                    icy scarification i know
          how we wake
                    each morning
                                        outside
          the eye the i the aye the (h)igh i
          open   palpable

                    . . . mo(u)rnin . . .

wait a minute! ent is my turn! mo(u)rning yet!

                    . . . mo(a)nin . . .

          is i, rie, wha speakin no . . . ow oh
          wan! two! tree! an' de winnah is . . .
          AS FOR YOU, mAri, YOU SUPPOSE TO BE SLEEPING . . .
          well well, good morning all! or is it moaning? anyway
          who sketched us in where
                    so many spare . . .

                         have any of you noticed

in the sick room   light
withers   still flowers shine
loft small buds to life
                    in udder words
time to rise an' shine . . .
          penelope is right, is especially sad now things so dangerous. but
allyouso ain't have no discipline. is big trouble coming . . .

is why pen-e-lope callin sheself cow? ah nevah . . .

SIGH cough sigh sigh . . . cut off their tails with a carving knife
have you ever seen such a thing in your life
   three blind mice gigglegiggle four blind mice giggle four blind
giggle giggle gigglegiggle mice . . .

   . . . ms lancet? yuh hear dat?
   mAri, rie, penelope, i calling all of you to pray with me.
jesus mary and joseph, we pray you to look on us with charity.
behold the cross of the lord.
             begone infernal enemies . . .

                . . . jahmin

jahmin, i've been sitting here for three hours, perhaps four. perhaps twenty.
i no longer remember. at least i still recognize the rooms. it's time, really,
that escapes me. but i'm not sleeping well. there is a baby in the building
seems to spend much of his time crying. i spoke to my doctor recently.
sounds like he lost my file or something. anyway he wants me to come
back in for a checkup. as if i'll even think about it! haven't heard from Bro
Jim for ages. i was quite thrilled for him. real success is so rare! plus he
can never be convicted of giving into the enemy! must be nice for him.
how's his lady wife taking it? she never even wrote to tell me. all these
pages! i must have worked all night. i'm tired enough! i'm sending you
everything. if you ever work out what they're about so much the better.
the only thing i can think of is automatic writing.

love even to the undeserving
                       who know who they are!
penny

Penny Performs

dear jahmin

what's your obsession with news?

USA BOMBS TOBAGO: BEACHES AMERICAN INTERESTS

CHRETIEN SCOOPS ASIAN NATIONS AWARD:
1998 HOST OF THE YEAR

ANIMAL RIGHTS ACTIVISTS FEED MASTER CHEF TO LION:
"ENDANGERED SPECIES NEED REAL MEAT"?

love

penny

Penelope Performs

dear jassy

Marilyn said, "Tell me. Right to the end."

She was in a single room. they were going to let her go. what day is it? they'd asked, and i swam up quickly, the others pushing me on, guessed, "thursday." what's your name? who's your doctor? how old are you? your address? where do you work? we'd answered them all. casual, quick. wanting to get out of there. to get out immediately. before they took something else.

now we stand at marilyn's office window staring at the red brick bulk the cream roof of the general rising through poplars, remembering. "there was pain. i was drowning in it, coming up for breath. i remember the helplessness. the body occupied. i remember the child pressing and moving. push, the body ordered, push. trying to hold on. the pain. my mouth, a wide screaming. pain and the sudden release. but the body's memory holding for a minute or five. then i myself, waiting the afterbirth. i even remember signing the papers, 'though what they said . . . i assume i've signed away the child?

Marilyn saying, "There's only a signature for new treatment. They really did show me all the papers."

silence.

"One of my friends . . . look, you've said your baby was a girl."

yes.

"The only black child registered that week was a boy. A good professional family adopted him. They've lived in Africa . . . but that's nothing to do with you. A male child."

what do you expect me to do now. flat.

"Now, don't hold back. Not on rage or grief. What I've told you is true. Accept it."

true She hadn't needed a psychiatrist to tell her that. i said nothing about the child crying giggling singing in her head. naturally, i said nothing about us, She was never going back into a canadian hospital.

i wept with abandon. with relief. as if we believed . . .

. . . jass, mAri here, pen-e-lope do real good. she bettah here dan in trini wha with de acksent an' thing. she belong dis climate. cool. is ice i mean here . . .

                . . . CLAP CLAPCLAPCLAPCLAP . . .
. . . slight tongue tight throat
      reflected in spring runoff
withered trees dream green
     zzzzzzzzzzzzzzzzzzzzzzzz

of such interruptions our lives are made

love

penelope

Penelope Performs

jassy

do not sing to you again
songs of sad penny?

> particular life needs particular space
> no doubt one as roomy sweet and meaty
> as a mango-vert not out of place

even one's own life's an enigma
how should i know?

still anything for you jassy

> i'll push
> sister kin

consider the calgary cabbie

> the small moments that make his day

out of bed   bear struck
by chinook sky   wary smile
at the wife

street's in slush and like some lives

> full of pedestrians

toss the baby
her first taste of flying

                    (soon you'll be able say who addicted you?
                    ME? outrage perfected
                    MY WHOLE LIFE FOR YOU!)
the rush

                        delicious fear
                    of ceilings   this tingle
                                and not knowing
                                    the safe
                    unsafe male hands
                    hard wired into her neurons
                the boy a thundercloud gone to his mother
leave wet towels everywhere don't bother
to grab a coffee slam into cab drive nowhere
                    wait for time's small change
slush
damn chinook
                    seventy minutes stretched to horizon
                        to india/kenya/b.c. the framed degree

God clearly knows your name your place
even the lame pick up their beds
to walk away
                        (hallelujah
stand fees   insurance   maintenance

time melting a long slow runoff

three co-op calls   round the block
                            (claim you can't find the fourth
    a lunch drunk
    a no show
     fare without a watch
    coffee

find a washroom
   wait at the ranks
stare as the people walk
                walk on by hum mm mmm
thrust your head into balmy wind hum
    these heels are made for walkies
don't think of gas school outing
   food
bank
   your father now there was a real man bless him
right and bright
      rent
    the blasted washing machine
       WATCH THE SPEED! BRAKE AND take a. . . !
    read king
  short trip 7 blocks on 9th ave
  talk radio bollocks! read king
coffee pour some over
back bumper
          christen the cab christine
slush

   3:30 pick up boy
  shed the raven
nice nice dad
          this kid's gonna starve

try the palliser hotel
  crowd on steps
    blessed anxiety
      rush the slush
airport! imagine
       that fare back

finally possibility   the day
  busted open
            despite slush
blasted wind
  blasted dispatcher
      blasted people walking
in sweetly warm alberta breeze

thank God for tourists
thank God for the japanese!

love

penelope

PS eastern domes   river   bluff   bridges   sky   bank towers still
  here   as well as

                spring poplars
                stick insects brooding
                congregation

oops! jassy wants reality; slap your wrist, girl!

Penelope Performs with mAri

dear jassy

it had to be done. we did it, mAri and i. each taking a turn as circumstances
dictated. it's all true really, one way or another. but i intend only to . . .

. . . traveller riding the tale
                             behold rwanda's bleeding moon
        mirrored in kosovo's rivers alert to far bland smiles
        lies in/difference the wind lifts its trailing gown hurries
        on look traveller where the woman walks round 'n' around
                             pounding the small flat then
        round
                    and around
                         down the first shallow stair where
        puddling bulbs reveal a beggar legs stunted to anger/fear
        his bowl of coins clinking he circles in back-hinged to a
        beat i blossomed like a flower and now am withered away
                         you are a vine that sheds unripened
round
            and around
                         dark-outside treetops cloud together
        above them thunderheads trail dark longfingered contracts
        guns/missiles/tanks/mines here and there a flare of cash
        moonlight shapes the gourds fallow in the field to a flare of skulls
        starred biz is biz Job is jobs and what if they are swept
                             away utterly like their own dung
round

and around

                              hurrying on
in the bow shimmering spears
    red   green   blue
       wait   with something other
               a third stair here something wrapped
                    a bundle stick as handle
                 odour of thick desire a wail
            burrowing something which like
      murdered mahogany turns liquid betrays grain knot craft
    a decade's polish centuries' certainty to slip slide crawl
towards its own gethesemane
   round
       and around
                 in dark-outside stars throw off all
           claim fall fall almost at the feet of lawns
       fall think what it is to lie for years and years with
                    the same square inch of grass
        and pause
round
     around
             down the fifth stair where yellow air hacked
              to iceberg opens seals shivering
                to shrugged indifference
      wound in the wall of this towering silence that wound
    reopened with studied innocence
  faith stumbles against the lintel
uncharitable in its easy yielding

traveller look the dark-outside
         look where now she goes stars hovering at her ankles
            a woman out of time moving as we move

in desperate moments   across some other ground
woman with her spiralling shock of hair
woman her hair like noon drizzle
captured not quite captured
by the black square
woman with guava tongue
woman with razor grass tongue
teeth like ivory o
lips like ripe jamaica plum
lips sweet as tulum
zipped to silence   her eyelids lift above eyes sudden
as tropical night
eyes like dew on a crow's wing
woman with her sapling neck
woman with her coconut breasts
watch her   that woman o
searching the midnight streets
for the smallest line of shadow   her
black synthetic overalls lean
into hedges into doorways
a woman without forensic fibres
she enters the boles of trees
with her caura valley waist
with her caroni delta hips
watch her deer-leap
the useless punctuation   green
yellow   red of one a.m.
crossings now the towers long
behind her she moves up centre street
moves towards the north
star on on through danger of bright
restaurants   car dealers   donut shops
pass SAIT its red brick grey

concrete patchwork   its rim of slender poplars
its institutional lawns   all this clear
on ruby r's map   now squiggled on our cortex
and she is cortez sailing past
crescent heights its rapunzel-let
let-down-your-hair turrets
its rounded windows
its night opulence
shadowed by older trees   she hugs
to herself their quiet living
watchfulness thinks of the child
his butterfly breath   his tight
sleeping hears his sudden thin mewl
watch her pause and straddle streets
that woman o
holding like an owl to the kill
that woman watch her turn
on crowchild trail pass mcmahon
watch her go boldly
her moko-jumbie legs
her shabby sneakers
black chew up the world between
her and the child
at hill top plaza her eyes rake the space
its bright fronts its dark patches
the sci fi faces of surfeited custom
under dim orangey glow her eyes from donut shop
back to yucatan's   now like an oil slick
her shadow to the cars   gloved hand
no stick shift no
or endless backing up
or narrow turnings but power steering
her lower lip between her teeth   seventh try

lucky now and only one swift dive to safety
this woman the congo rising in her navel
puts on a straight short greying black wig
no hint of curl to mark her
to this a pair of large round glasses
a blood red scarf streaked white
and black like a noose around her neck
how now she passes over
how now her flesh slips softens around her
she turns the careless key slips
slides calmly quietly from the lot
and so past night clubs cafes
out on to crowchild to shaganappi
obedient to traffic lights just
slightly over speed limits any
grandma returning to her soft quiet room
after a noisy evening of babies
or a woman gently from her lover
she turns left onto dalhousie
moves easily   coming where
heart's-home on steep hills coming
where her fly-back-to-guineablood coos
burbles its command on dalton drive
far from machetes kitchen knives hoe-handles
whips tender bullets far from squeezed screams
shock the tight-coiled terror of hiding
here relatively safe   relatively free she drives
straight past the house we seek
to the next crescent
parks the car steps out
look traveller look where a taxi o
slips in behind her   a man shovelled out
a driver swearing in hindi and english

her feet already on driveway she
walks straight up the path God help her   he follows
calls in a hoarse whisper
"good night" and she pauses calls
back does not turn necessity
throttling her   she lifts a gloved hand
waves right royally   walks
on and around the house listening his footsteps
she leans   deep breaths of early summer growing
a long minute against the back wall
then completes the circuit he wavers
weaves uncertain on the top step   damning
shitting the keys which will not obey
his fingers
which fall from his hand
he scrambles grasping after
cursing the blown bulb while
she moves swift   traveller   look how
she heels for the near corner   fades
in the dark how she is caught
by this other drama pauses to watch
      while he
      his mouth working dismally
      turns   shifts   looks around
      zig zags across his lawn
      crosses to the car we parked
      chuckles   pats the smooth sides
      chuckles   reaches in
      triumphant
      stumbles up the drive
      scrambles up to lean
      against the door
      glares at the keys

chooses
brow furrowed he
    tries the lock
    tries the lock
  jabs at the lock
       pauses looks up
a dark window
tries again
and again
   again
whispers shSheila shSheilll?   SSHHHHEILAaaAH shhSHEILAAH? open
up Sheil please Sheil
   next door a window
    a volley of curses
  the window slams
  he waits long minutes
  Sheilee? open please
   please a whisper
back at the lock
      until
slowly carefully
infinitely gently he
  aims his key turns
the door pushed open
  he chuckles looks around
stares at the car
chuckles
finger to his lips
shshshshshhhhh
he scrawls inside

now she sighs
  sighs

now lean and hard again sticking to shadows
that woman with a volcano in her belly
that woman with spears in her eyes
moves sinuous silent down dalton street
her nose sniffing the wind   her child
its scent in a dark garden she moves sure
to stand beneath the second window
on the second floor

. . . traveller look to the north sky   it is the second hour
see there that cloud at right sky empty of stars
there now look how it shapes a world
        read it traveller
                            find what suits you
            what you need
                                    so all men read . . .

SILENT MOVIE

Night

1. Dalhousie. Two a.m. A heavily treed middle class suburb built on steep hills. View of the downtown lights, towers, from a great distance. The suburb itself is relatively poorly lit. And abed.

2. In darkness, a large split-level house on a sloping corner lot. The entrance to the house is lit by a sixty-watt carriage lamp. Small front lawn. Large poplar to the right. To the left, clump of small pines. Adjoining double garage to the left, its doors electronically stuck at the halfway mark. An Audi barely discernible in the dark. There is a red Honda in the driveway.

3. Occupants of house. A man, his wife, a small baby, nanny. Very dim light shows through screens of one window.

4. Back view of the house. A patio of crazy paving covers most of the back yard which is surprisingly level. A narrow oblong patch of grass surrounded on two sides by narrow beds of vegetables and flowers. A seven-foot cedar fence surrounds the entire back yard. Two gates, one to the front lawn, right, and one to the back lane. Barbecue, patio furniture, a bunny wading pool, other items de rigueur to Calgary back yards. Light above back door.

5. Androgynous hooded figure dressed all in black. Quick practised movements. Bent double, figure runs across garage roof to dimly lighted window. Gloved hands lift screen out, set it down.

6. Bedroom next door to nursery. A woman in a flannel night dress buttoned up to the neck is lying very still. A man removes his pyjama jacket, smiling ingratiatingly, and drops it on the floor. He continues to strip slowly. The woman never takes her eyes from his face. She does not smile.

7. A plane, pre-Second World War, helmeted pilot leaning over side, begins to circle the house, to drop thousands of tiny pieces of paper, jaggedly torn. The face is indistinguishable. The plane is quite high up. Nevertheless the paper falls only on this house. Paper like snow drifts/blows throughout the scene.

8. The figure at the window pours a thin stream of oil from a tiny can into the grooves, slides window back and begins to climb in.

9. Bedroom. Man pulls top sheet off woman. Without moving her head, she fixes her eyes on a statue of the Virgin Mary straight ahead of her. She is lying like a corpse. Hands folded over her breast. The man no longer smiling. Eyes like lasers. He gestures to her to lift her nightdress. She does not move.

10. Interior of dimly lit nursery. Decorations by Disney Studios. Figure stands as if in a trance against the wall near the window. Close-up of face. Eyes glued on crib in centre of room. Lips parted. Through bars a slow zoom to tiny African baby asleep on its side. Black hair spirals away from a bare spot on the scalp. Legs move slightly under the covers. Wide angle to whole room. Figure snaps out of it, looks around quickly, noting placement of furniture etc.

11. Nursery. Figure moves calmly towards crib, bends over, lifts baby, tucks it into black cloth carrier, baby gives small cry of discomfort. Figure darts towards crib, picks up teddy, freezes. Listens. Teddy into pack. Turns quickly towards window. Baby begins to squall.

12. Hall. Stairs lead down to a railed landing. A woman, angry, runs up stairs, grabs nursery door knob, turns it, opens door.

13. Nursery. Figure crouched behind large upholstered rocker in corner near window. Door opening.

14. Hall. Muffled sound. Woman startled, pauses as if listening, She looks in direction of bedroom.

15. Nursery. Baby squalling through muffling hand.

16. Hall. Woman in doorway, still looking along hall, frowning.

17. Nursery. Crouched figure begins to rise slowly. Kitchen knife caught in light. Baby squalling.

18. Hall. Muffled cursing from bedroom, stifled squeal. Woman turns suddenly. Creeps down hall. Listens. Cautiously begins to open door. Hesitates. Looks toward nursery.

19. Bedroom. Man riding nanny who is arched toward him. Legs clasped over his back. Her head thrown back, she is screaming into the flannel nightgown. Sudden light.

20. Nursery. Figure half in half out of window. Hand protecting child's head.

21. Bedroom. Camera caresses woman standing in doorway, hand on the light switch. She begins to walk towards the bed.

22. Bedroom. Wide-angle shot of room. The woman is still walking towards the bed. A pair of pyjamas is draped over the Virgin.

THE END

don't like the resolution, jassy?

                        prefer love?

tender as a peach
dark as midnight
striding steep cliffs
the rapids and rocky fastnesses
sun-dappled green air
of the congo   its jungle
awake and roiling
to his whistle

or should it be hate?
            (the horror, the horror
caged beast turning frost-white
crouches on narrow boards
yellow eyes singe
the air as his breath
cracking the dry earth
promises and nothing live after me
the tall woman striding on the river's bank!

okay then try this

22. Telephoto shot of World War 1 plane. Pilot is tossing tiny bits of paper from his window. He circles house once, then zooms to window.

23. Bedroom. Wide angle shot of room. Nanny-woman on the bed looks around wildly. Sees plane. Stops moving abruptly.

24. Pilot flaps his wings.

25. Wife-woman turns her head sharply, sees the plane. Stares. Her frozen face begins to dissolve. The camera moves quickly to the bed before we can be sure whether she laughs or cries.

26. Pilot wiggles his ears. He does a roll.

27. Nanny-woman throws the man off in one sudden strong movement. Steps on his body, climbs on the sill, straddles the window.

28. The pilot lends a wing.

29. The man lies on the bed, eyes bulging, complete disarray.

30. Wife-woman rushes across room, steps on man, grasps wing.

31. The pilot shrugs elaborately. Wife-woman climbs through and onto the plane.

32. Camera circles the room. Dishevelled. Empty despite man on bed. Pyjama pants on one outstretched Virgin arm, night gown hangs from the other.

33. Pilot takes off. Wife-woman holding to the roof, one foot on the wing, gown billowing behind her. Nanny-woman lying on the nose, head up. As still as death, except for her eyes.

34. Man rushes to window.

35. Camera follows as plane zooms up. Rolls a salute. Climbs into wild blue yonder.

35. Camera looks down on the house and yard. In the shadows a black figure, barely distinguishable, a baby carrier heavy on her chest, flits towards the road.

THE END

love

penelope
and mAri

Penny Performs

dear jahmin

you thought poetry was marked by precision? well . . .

Conceptual Poem: Sonnet

woman with parrot

the dissembling bed

the ocean

God dreaming as usual

love

penny

Rie Performs

lo mina

in plain english yuh wan' trut'?
yuh sistah come de Bow now tell mi
is why yuh doan like poetree?
is how yuh tink i tell bout we
in t'ree line an' does yuh like mi rhyme?

yuh ent know mem'ry like dem ditch flower
gorn seedy   root it out   it doan dead
drip poison it grown back maad   is weed
is hydra head   She look
in mirror who know wha She-so see?

buh is why yuh doan tell we how
de lan lie? an' wen las yuh
tayse coconut pie, cachourie or
a sweet lime? gurl here is to pine
ah dyin to see a poui
white aripo in a meadow
macaw in a chataigne
so long since i see calypso
or jump up in a hot tent to wine
mi body-line

if yuh wan' know de Bow flow slow
murky   full a slime an' who to say
wha else hidin below?

by de way before i go
de gurl ha a bout o' blight
de chile undo She skin thin
we slide out She pore

is de inside wha leakin out
it ent ha nutten sneakin in

as yuh mus know dat ha big big flaw
nobody in charge   is show
widdout star barge sans captin

pr'haps de Bow doan flo so slow

love gurl

rie

Penny Performs

dear jahmin

a rose by any other name
would smell as sweet

how could it not knowing
rose not knowing sweet?

love

penny

The bell of apartment 831 rang as if it sounded in a vast hollow space. At least it wasn't musical. She waited twenty seconds and pressed it again.

"Hello! How are you? And who is this?" She stooped, tall, angular, white hair, and cooed.

"Just wanted to check that we weren't disturbing you. This is Charlie! My sister's kid. He's holidaying while they're on a cruise."

"Look at him! What a lovely boy you are! Come in for a minute. I'm in the den."

"Thanks! Just for a minute, though. He's going to start howling soon."

"So you've had visitors. I thought you might have!"

"Nothing like sisters. They flew in, stayed a couple of days, fussing like a couple of hens."

"And your roommates?"

"They're back. Shushh, Charlie, ssssshhh! Come on baby, come on! Well, now you've really met!"

"Healthy lungs!"

"Quite the roar! Perhaps he'll be a singer! Poor boy, he's hungry! We've got to go!"

"Amazing aren't they? Not sleeping through the night yet, is he! How much longer do you have him?"

"Her doctor says she needs a month!"

"Ah! Post-natal blues!"

"Husshhh, baby! We must be going! See you!"

Penny Performs

dear jahmin

today sky sprawled blue over jet trails through
glass the character tock tock shaping
swish and spling of living washed to greyish
hum and distance so plump sparrows
building a drainpipe nest their chitter and squawk
become anchor you remember don't you
how mid-may's northern noon clouds
memorial poplars blues certain pines
flattens all colour clears streets
lawns of shadow now even the bow
glimmers only where it bunches raw silk
flung carelessly through our city's centre (i
know you too have seen this but listen)
today this little air weft
to warp of spare light among leaves shapes
tree tips to swift slivering beauty   and i find myself
clinging as if my bare feet clenched
high to rock-face the grip slip-sliding
so though i want to tell you how your niece
melted at my breast   rapt to the old eve
how her eyes shone into my own how clearly clean
warm we felt inside this enriching arc
how sweet her lips and chin (more like mum's
every day) the very air fracturing slips between
and i know myself trapped half here
                              half some else where

jahmin quicksand and i old pals

but i remember bruised mangoes in rough-tongued grass pale gecko's
tloc tloc the lamp's leap and flare as river wind searched our hair blessed
our skin all this even then gathered   held hard   while words like steps
to night's veranda invited and charmed   one ancient aunt or another
drunk on the tale its telling   wove rooms cupboards forest trails alleys
where yellow red blue possibilities glowed shifted greyed while
mosquitoes sawed their mocking music despite coils citron and we
clapped slapped punctuation beneath brilliant stars   in such deep
nights in such dense country   fusion

                    here no aunts no stars
          not a one
                              as if hubris had put out a million
million eyes with blade and spoon
                              i smell a lear here but
                              the gods are just and of our virtues make
the spear that shakes us

                         help then! send some story i can
use to arm Charla against the gimme gimme lure of things
the frantic thrashing of desire a story to show how you can't
play sailor if you 'fraid powder how the whole world it nothing
but one marshy sea & the sea ain't got no back door . . .
                              in truth it's worse   that my edges
spill beyond thick black lines
              blur into dream
                         whirl
                              that like a green girl
or an amoeba
i slow
          to indifferent directions

i don't know
whose child or why but I fear first my face like lace
                    then a fading
to negative space

one)   all here outlined in thick black paints at
                                            the moment
two)   so are my lineaments through ragged black
                                                    lines
                            from nose to mouth
three)   the child still screams for her story
                                                possibly
                        preferring milk but i have none
four)   tell the brothers of this and i shall curse you
                                        beyond eternity
five)   seeing as mean eye is the mean   i mean that

if
(even if)
it be true Lord
(you lift the darkness)
transcendence stick in us
        the lonely horn soloing spirals
(only in us this grand gift)
still in the end shroud ain't have
(o child shout all you want   shroud can't)
        piano pinging in
                        drums spatter and stammer
(it ain't have)
  pocket know you
(kno-o-ooo-oow)
  know shroud
  ain't have pocket

(you gotta gotta gotta know)
there ain't no shroud with pocket
(no-no-nooooo no)
horn rushing down stairs
no way out
(no way ouououout aw aw out)
Lord knows
  (Lord knows)
        horn its wailing
                baffled into expectant silence
                        the final drawl

might you be able to work up a tune for this?
i've got another: who put the tam in tamboo bamboo?
we could change it to the "bam" if you prefer?
no? then jahmin team up please
perhaps among our childhood's rubble
in that bruised eden at lopinot or floating
a bright feather above the middle passage's miasmas
find a tale shield before soul
                a small raincoat
      for life
                size five months
or at least
                a row boat

in your letter you say you sometimes wonder about me. shouldn't
that be wander? and in any case, why?
                        as for the rest
here is your note tossed back
ere the tongue flare

on this austere morning further
smear the glass we are not kinder
not kinder either
what? german of course!
                    i shall use what i care to
of your letter
the point of a secret: the delight
full sharing

                                        my letters are different

summer lightning flickered
in my bones last night
                              also
even in her sleep
your niece quickened to it
                              also
in the co-op a man insists
my doppleganger again
                              also
this morning the paper
flower boomed
                    white

                              do not ask what
a paper flower is (poem origami
wait for it . . . bougainvillea?) nah!
nor b-o-o-m   listen
                    the heavy oo tolling
oo oo oo oo marking the century
near enough
(it is true
              i'm humorous

a laugh a decade that's me)

i smell a metaphor burning
time to switch off the stove

PS   Why can't i write letters like other people? philistine!
PS   Why won't i write poems like other people? hell's gate. and get
published!
PS   i am nothing
            even with daring doubles
so do nothing

                        this afternoon
                        i shall strip
                        to solitude
                        do ye like wise
                                    perhaps then a story
                                            on the edge of consciousness
                                        like a haunt
            or a consolation

            moon
huge as a yawn
ravening
between poplars

i shall write no more till you send a tape of the tale
do not try to lure me out
                    your flies gaudy as christmas

PS   how many letters i write each week? how many i send?
        with a kid? don't be feeble!
PS   do i have a nanny? why?

plus
    only a sister sniffs vanity all around
plus
    you asked me to send yer man a truly decent book, didn't
    you, didn't you? what's wrong with shakespeare? fanon? achebe?

PS another day another $ . . . if you're a poet
    a dollar's a wonderful surprise

             and yet
this morning's light
the taste of bread
dipped in virgin oil/vinegar
do you remember?
paprika's sweet sharp bitter
all scattered by the scalding chitter
of sparrows i step into the balcony's cool
a cloudburst the river silvering
but inside me
dark water glistens rises
with it whisperings tongues
thrusting at my throat
    i choke on . . .

still the child
who is the long wind's wet fingers shivering at my hair
who is also the bed hard and empty even of the lover's scent
who is already a memory   but sharp edged
       and oh . . . my sudden body breaks into leaf
into branch . . .
         splash

                splash
splash . . .
    and then the dishes
the laundry
            vacuum spills
beds   dust
    snack toilets
put the child down
pick the child up
            play with the child
        wipe up pick up
                lay the table
stir the jam
                not that i make any
except here of course
            still
        prepare
            bottle
        store baby food
wash up
wash up
. . . the child
        the child
such mewling

                but why am I telling you
            sister you know
                all this I am the neophyte here
                so tired trying so hard to walk
        in holiness
well when i think of it, of course!

do not look to my lips for yer mother

meanwhile

I shall hound you down the fax
and down the phone
I shall hound you in your neighbour's sax
and though you bound
                    and race
                            and hide
I shall hound you in the tide

remember I
            WE come for Christmas!
            does simonette still chill
every night his horn
            as if he were the last man
                            on earth
                    moon
                    or no moon?

INCIDENTALLY THIS IS NOT BULLYING
you are being silly about the price of fax paper and the answer
to your last question: any sweetly intelligent person!

PS sky arcing an eyelid
        scotsman's bluff
        the high naked cheek bones

finally, jahmin . . .

every day's light seeps in
her skin translucent
as if neon sun halogen moon
stars satellites
   beep and bop through her pores   a shadow
                    She writes: i love mommy
                                 daddy too

. . . jass gurl yuh ent know is how long She sit here an' de chile ent feed
plenty talk buh is penelope an miz lancet wha look aftah chile . . .

i'm still here in the pleated
circle we fan out
when you least expect
at midnight a naked foot hung
               lavender and pearls   thinned
                    She writes: i love baby
                           and Thena-Marie
stippled concrete sky lit don't
think of tears on their hinges
laughter's scrawl
scenting roses corners doors
slammed between honey on hot bakes
blunts nothing fading
                  She writes: i love sister
                        i think i love me

got you going didn't i! aren't words marvellous? this morning a
bouquet of scented red roses and baby's breath. lovely. it quite
perked me up. from someone called mAri. no idea. but i do think the
spelling intriguing.

love

penny

Ms Lancet and Marie Performs

Conversation

but why She showing the child around so? She ain't read the paper, or what? they searchin every whichwhere for chile!

Miz lancet, is sorry i so sorry fuh dat pore mudder!

rie, is we Charlie dey lookin for? beside, ent is de mudder gie he up for doption? moreso he black. doption famly white-white. deyso ent know wha dey getting into.

mArie that's essentialist nonsense! besides, how much longer do you think it will be before they get here?

a long time. She done establish de chile belong She sistah. all wha She need is plane crash. yuh tink anybody here goin doubt She?

Penny Performs

dear jahmin

i am not what i am
says iago

who am i
when i am not i?
says   penny-marie lancet

and why is jahmin?

love

She

Ms Lancet Performs

jasmine child

           here we trying to chink the worl'
with callaloo fried plantain barefoot rice an' foo-
foo to make a rope wit' succoyant whine   papa
bois bamboo tamboo   use tenor pan riff & caiso to
twine the whole we mould
                                 hope
                       foolish pride
      to make
                to frame
   child
            find a calabash
                burnt gourd scored
            with red jasper   from where these hang
       press up against night's shank
                       grasp one
    with both hands you needing
              its half light to drink . . .

. . . jass before de face o' Gawd
      mirror her akan or yoruba
a great tree sucklin wisdom we children slidin through
white space lef' wit'in   between   beyon'
                     story)
   buh here
       at winter out/skirt
on blue midnight's balcony

portion o' dis body dis instrument
i siddown now in/habit myself
back here under nordern lite . . .

                    . . . child
              we offer you not only this messy century's red an'
                                        poison images
                         but something else
                  stranger sweeter more difficult
            until our face   various
                         brims at rim of bowl
                                        of calabash . . .

                    and now
      now and
                              now jasmine
      is rough sea and story come seeah! allyouso seeah! it have
      a woman it have four selfs four lands a woman family of
      lancet it have a child and it have a kinda life a scream what
      come to you whole   desert you stumble into even so before
      you could cry out   wind's knife   whip sand in heavy torrents
      light   you   scrambling for footing   in depths
                    dunes
            sun caves
                                   giant arabesques
                  in dread
        then trees mirage of cliff blue oases horizontal
        line and youself   thing what carry
                                   slow waves
                    what ride

hard

                          sun-shaped

      angles

                                             honed

sun feeding even in hollows sun scalping veins
glazed forehead ahead of you white skull bright
bone trailed a light house fallen on sand scattered on
scrub it still pulses low warning

                            then again allyou
it have a kinda living some kinda experience
it come in broke   time splintered glances on youself
and you a reproach driven back   the world come

                      j

                                                      i

  g

                                  s

                    a
                        w

lef' to you faint feints

                      slender afternoons hurrying here there
dreams games revolts a puppeteer   blank encounters stretch down long
hours   all of it all nothing   jest an alphabet toss an' scatter on the
floor   take a lifetime to tease out link touch with glance here event
there dream wit' word to code a life its defiant grammar

     but this it worse

                  a kind what have no beginning
                  no ending

                                          youso
                      you pull a thread

unravel

the world . . .

. . . where time's prism fragments

reality

its fierce colours mock
our dim dailiness
we to memory as a toddler to wild rocking horse . . .

. . . COUGHcoughsigh . . . mummy's got a bunting rock an rock
an all FALL DOWN . . .

. . . ms lancet wha wid de rockin' horse?
mAri, i ain't know. we hear her before.
yuh still don' tink it could be She?
but is not those two others? sound like them to me, the
last little chile. and the first one don't sound like She either.
allyou dere? hey, is how yuh doin'? i'm mAri. hellooo?

. . . zzzzzzzzzzzzzzzzzzzzzzzzzzzzzzzzz
giggle giggle giggle . . .

mAri, perhaps She bound to crack up?
ms lancet, yuh ha to fin' out, yuh bettah wid chile
dan me. i really really hope She ent gorn mad. allyuh
hear wha in dat gigglin?
penelope?
ms lancet, it's not i. we've just got to wait, i think.
don't believe it's She. no self-control for one thing.
rie?
not me! an 'nodder ting, we ha' dis agreement wit' She.
deyso na in it.

i better finish my letter, yes. but i think we must pay
attention. all-a-we is to pray, yes.
drown we in drug an' say dey savin' we.
right! as ms lancet said, we stay on our toes. No rest
for the wicked.
yeah! let we cliche fo'ward on de quiet an' pdq!

jahmin
                        listening before the line
                            look into your bowl
            see where the clot
                    stops this seam
                                            n   a
                        where time u   d   l   n
                                              u   t
is undone
                unduly
                        is formed
                                    deformed
in to history . . .

. . . i i i am penny penny penelope-marie/up a tree/pray for me
penny penny-marie . . .

. . . coughsigh . . . mummy's going to buy you a mockING BIRD
                                    gigglegiggle . . .

st anthony, beloved patron of lost things, help us. help please. i know
i lose mi way. god help us . . . anyway jasmine girl is i marie lancet where
bow and elbow river meet april making cold rainy the trees aint have full
leaf . . .

. . . poplars foam black
        the shore stifles masterful

names runed ruined . . .

so it come all along them river banks shallow hills it have every kind
of new green daubing stick-brown lawn leafless tree the bow with this
crashing untidy sky saying more an' what it say patchy pewter we here
corralled not jes' by bluffs

> . . . glass city balancing
>   its trick tricycle
> prairie awry coattails
>   sprawl to windswirled
> distance Calgary grown
>   past virgin cowboy
> come to town . . .

look, penelope, i tell allyou already, you want to write She, write She.
i fed up with allyouso interrupting. you behavin like you drag up in
some gutter . . .
    well, pardon me, ms lancet. but i know how jassy loves this city . . .
the whole thing its sweeping sculpture of bridges across time rivers
warehoused lives across the thirties & forties still crouched in small
gardens on river-strips below steel and glass pyramids our new
cathedrals all this thrust into remembrance of poplar/small-water/sky/
grassy bluffs all squeezed there in flat light knotted in the lie of
perspective spewing the gray sweat of eunuchs and so ms lancet i beg
your indulgence . . .

> . . . mina gurl
> but is why allyou can't hear?
>   jes' dis miz lancet an' i gorn
> undah cross an' dome
> below arro-gant sky lines
> of discarded eyes. . .

jasmine
    below the hiss and grind of traffic   below the wind
beyond the rim of dreams . . .

child it have a kind of silence to prison in. i supping on misery here, but under this sky i can't be alone with it. is angle of light what making me see meself in the glass, but only from the shoulder down. i see meself standing there holding Charlie, waiting. i say he name, he move against me. i open up She japanny dressing gown what have the lotus flower sleeves the one you send She. i open down to the bikini. i hold him against skin. he turning his dark head a little as he always do. i watch him in the glass, an' i watch the woman that i suppose is me. dark as dark in the early light. i watch the way you watch a ghost: she lift the child away from her body like she 'fraid he touch. she grab the crimson gown closed with one hand. is blurry in folds till she settle the chile tight to she neck, and stand there swaying. tall, slim, hard. except where she soft. about Charlie, girl i don't know. and it ain't have nothin' so bad as not knowing

this ain't the beginning of course. no kind of beginning. in the beginning was the word. a thing people always quoting, its easy superiority. grandeur, i suppose. in She case the word is baby-sister . . .

             . . . we who are female know
       our entry on the lattice of time
                                  the will to thrust
       and thrust through dark unknowing
                                only then the small tongue
       writhing lip cough & startle into
                             scream
       afterwards
                 long succession
                         secession of OH OWWWWS
       interweaving of laughter
                       prayer
               the soft brown ground of contentment
           the long autumn of remembering
       and curving space   till
                             OhOHOH gasp OOOOOH . . .
                             till oh oh . . .

. . . coughcough time fell down an' broke his crown
an' hope came TUMBLING after
  giggle gigglegigglegiglegigle giggle . . .

penelope?   dis ent no adventure   dis is bad bad trouble
                    OOWWWW . . . gasp . . . O!! GAAAWD . . .

but is how long i standing here? i can't stand here all day, you know, i got
to get dressed. our grandmother tell She "you face anything if you dress in
your pretty dandan." you growin' up is hard to make sense, to know what
matter. grand also use to say "people always get what they really want, is
how come the world full o' private hell." is to look at we crosses now!
    i turn from the window; Charlie make that mewlin' sound like i spoil his
view. i pat his back, sway a little bit and go "shush baby, shushushush."
then i begin to explain him everyting. i figure i owe him that. you know
with cyril how it so natural holdin' a baby. as if we body make for this an'
nothing else. he hush his chittering, settle heself back. he so separate, so
perfect, though he already have his little ways. i suspect is that perfection
She need. fresh crisp snow what nobody ain't walk on. She figure she get
another chance. She be Penny-Marie, of course, your sister. i be marie
lancet, and there's mAri, rie and penelope too. now we hear other voices.
She fraying real bad. it have bits and pieces. is a strange thing. is wonder
i wonder all the time how it is to be you one alone, the whole yourself,
a secure soul. but is not so with us. now we falling apart. each of we
thin, jagged, holding on by strand. is hard to function with memory like
a ragged vest, and is not easy either to stick to who you are. if anybody
does ever know that.
    well, i walk through the living room what really full up. is because
mAri buy new furniture she say african. i sure is siam, arms and legs
wrap with brass. i don't see how that go with penelope overstuff chairs,
an' She victorian chaise; the walls is something else. somebody paint one
dead black, all dem splash paintings, an' She serious bout twine an' tin
can! my Sacred Heart picture missing again. penelope always hiding it
behind the bookcase. i put Charlie down and take the time to hang it
up; this house need blessing more than ever. nobody 'cept me going to
church, mAri have she own god call obatala! say for african, africa god!
child, it ain't easy yuh know.

in the walk-in closet is jes' to stare at the clothes stuff up there. i got to work out what best for when police get here, because is come they coming sooner than later. i ignore all mAri stuff, what with big sleeve, dreads, she gowns, an' ting. that girl land up in africa they going to know immediately she american. i figure is also . . .

. . . mzzzz lancet, dem is de onliest decent clothes in de whole damn closet! . . . to ignore . . .

. . . Sheessssssssh . . .

all my decent ordinary dresses and what not in this rie like me only with her is jeans shirt sweaters she like tweed jsckets nothing fussy . . .

. . . EGGZACKLY! . . .

but i recognize this is time for silk and cashmere, what She does wear, or She good belgian linen what well cut. penelope does spend a fortune on clothes too. nothing but the best from the best stores. but hers all real casual she can't be bothered to dress up for nobody. you know, She always always wondering is why She can't resist sales when the closet packup with stuff She can't wear. a psychiatrist tell She once is She way of "releasing tension." i have to say mAri behave real good. she let the man talk he talk. sometimes is one set of inappropriate giggling mAri does put down. one thing She have going for She in this canada, is inventive She is, eh. real creative. besides we black. is a funny thing about racism here, lots of stuff you couldn't get away with in trinidad, here they ignore because maybe they think you don't know better. but is also they don't want to look racist! o well! back to the clothes. i don't want to go to no police station looking like they could push me 'round. still is not good to go flaunting yourself either. i doing all this one-handed and Charlie ain't like this closet at all at all. every time i step in is so he start with his fussing. anyway i reach over with one hand and pull out the rayon/linen blend with the soft cardigan and long swirling skirt, what peter always say She look romantic in. that poor man. is true he never say what he mean. but he never know really who he dating . . .

. . . he knew exactly whom he was dating. a woman of infinite variety . . . is opera/ballet is penelope. is disco an' any african art or entertainer is mAri. is endless talk and coffee shop is She. me, i invite him to church once twice he say he have to see he mother! ah well, is not like we could really afford good friend worse yet boyfriend. still, you don't want somebody like peter for your chile, if you understanding me. and if wasn't for him, we wouldn't be in this trouble now.

. . . that's silly he's not responsible for Charles, if there ever was a baby!

pssst pen-e-lope, whoever he tink he takin' out, is i de fun. . . . mAri funfunfun is all you ever think about isn't it? ms lancet is right!

penelope, yuh cyan even hear de riddems o' earth or relax to let music take yuh. dis is wha a body for. nex time yuh pick up dickshunary look up de senses!

you crapaud!

. . . SIGHgigglegigle mirror mirror on the wall
who is the giggle giggle giggle fairest . . .

oh lawd man! is why allyou can't be decent!
jasmine, is not like we could let She marry anyway. couple times we had to be real ruthless. was a matter of survival. anyway, anyway, in the end i decide on She linen jacket and skirt in plum and a grey silk shirt. i hide it far back in the closet so nobody wear it when i ain't here. now is time to feed Charlie i turn . . .

. . . i walk back through the dim hall to the bedroom crooning her name, dancing with her. God, i'm lucky mine! well . . . ours, i suppose ours. one thing we did well together, Charla, your dad and i, my darling baby girl, was dance . . .

jasmine child, i surface back to find Charlie screaming his lungs out, and She standing there staring at She-self in the mirror like She puzzle puzzle. She don't even hear him.

well, God bless girl! good luck with your new job, glad to hear you get somebody reliable for CLR. i've got to go now somebody got to feed this poor child.

. . . well now you know what
                  traveller lulled by the old
          securities expecting why
                  expecting how

          beneath your dream flag see it all
    (the woman split
                  the landscape of marvels

                        draw nearer

look how life prowls
wolf howling down the wind
bear scrunting in trees

love

marie lancet

Penelope Performs

in the elevator

"Hello, been shopping for the new addition?"
"Yeah, but he's only temporary. Slept the whole way through."
"Really cute! What's her name?"
"Boy! Charles, Charles Anthon."
"Anthon! Just unusual enough."

Penny Performs

dear jahmin

i walk through the valley
of wind tatters and eyes fingering

for you are with me

who? what?

love

penny

Ka'ci   Woman of the Arawak and the Karinabu/Carib
Performs her Sound/ing

jasmine   nutia'matu ilewe
        my pretty flower

for you   for her
this story
                            in the woman's tongue
                            no son would speak
nuwa'tu my fire
nukarre'hi my strength

once the island dreamt in my blood
tina the river swam in my eyes

the soft green hills
the blue world of sky and bara'wa

then this
ka'ci in a wild dance
no'nu flirting
in our skies

wa'cu wak u'kua ku'rapia'u
crayfish woodpigeon singing bird
waya'maka me'cu
iguana cat make small make still
                            dangerous voyages
the way of the world
and spiderwebs

before such shame we discover our faces
we peek between fingers
our bodies go their own way
                                        the earth trembles
            flourish of clouds
    moon smiles
            licks at the sun
                who stands
                    stunned
who flares out
        hopeful
                    there breaks held breath there slams heart racing
                                            indecipherable
                        to catch a ride on vastness

behind our faces
    the clicks and cries
                                this un(ac)countable fraying
        i admit
                                the way of flesh
                i would undo nothing

in the circle field
    grass bickers
    huts
        forest
    broken moans children
no'nu the moon
        bites
                        earth trembles
                        biriha'ali richa

lightning rears up
        the black axe falls

                      as if kuwi fish hook
                      naku the eye
                              open
around the sun nuku'suru he'hwe
my snake mother riffles her brilliant feathers

                a slow blood
   hya'mohya-ali
       and yes so cold

trees sway swallow my heart's
air branches claw in my chest
    i cling to the house post

             i am
                 uati
                 uati
           there is not

skipping down the mountains
                  spurt and   dr dr dr
                        ip ip op
a white rain
greasing the leaves the rocks
the beaten earth
      wind   children dogs
the sudden men stamping the sun into life
with rattles
with chac-chacs
with flutes

                    i join the ululation of women
                                with wielding
                        knife our own blood
        we paste and patch the world
                    flesh of one newly born
                            our own skin
            the crack sealed
            the world steadied

                                    or so it seemed where
deer worshipped karinabu/manicou called to dogs/from teasing bowers
a surf of cries laughter/fish craved nets/sons their lean brown bodies
stretched towards always/meanwhile daughters bloomed/dry-season
poui dreamt our shoulders/blue corn ripened early/in pots oil water/at
field's edge wood/honey poured from combs abandoned on stepped
branches/once crabs in fiery procession/once a child sang to us from
the womb/with this round expansion of bright fruits our circle dances
fluted leapt from dusk to dawn/while kiskadee and golden-headed
manakin nested together tumbled on high excited wings with the
ochre-bellied flycatcher/such soft fresh airs   sweet sweet water

                        O the joy/the joy/the joy

            first hunger fled then thirst we did as we must
                            we waited
                        singing our stories
            enjoy our eerie languorous longing

                    we surprise the fringes of self

three moons later
                winged sails
from the east
            sibilant bearded men

butterflies of death

laughing we gathered fruit
we greeted them welcome

iron flame

hammers
skulls   sickness
sudden
                  out of
season
                  gestures
                  mocking
savage

iatina suru makuiti i am a mother without a coffin
i do what mothers do
tu-ki ma-ku-ra'-ue   tu-ki ma-ku-ra'-ue
they make war 0 lazy one they make war 0 lazy one
bin-ha-ri ta-nu-ra man-ne-re im-u
unwilling thou to flee thou my son
ka-ima bi-ci-ka-ni ka-iwa-ku
come, take the lead come, wake up
ka-ima bi-ci-ka-ni ka-iwa-ku   (sung slowly sadly)
come take the lead come wake up

and so before the karinabu herded
and so to coarse cloth to blindfold

and choking   i he-re-tic
                  i mur-der-er
before their god
their black robes
their flames flirting with my hair
before my daughters

                              what i did not expect that sweet
                                        welcoming silence

i kariphu'ne   carib woman
                    glimpse her
i ka'buru   the mixed blood
tongueless
                    finally
i me'kuru   the negro

        now the sun daughter
                    weyu wuri
            now
            smooth black rich-tongued
                      i aim what i am
              i spread like best butter olive oil
              cocoa fat i seep through smooth i aim
            to please like corn coconut palm
                always available
                            in a lighter version

nunikua

i self
through the deep woods
ara'bsen
of time
nunikua
i myself
iwai'yu hurru
tempest

                                    i aim i
              naku my eye   naricae my ear
          nuracue my belly   nu'ruku
             my genitalia   i aim myself i
          tumble through   centuries
                    iatina   i am i self
               light as air   here home
          flesh of my flesh   ma'brika!
           which is to say   welcome
                    lakrea   which is to say
                            it is my wish
                                lakrea . . .

     . . . eh well! i like how you talk your talk. a real live carib queen!
   we do not have queens. once we were warriors. how it has rained on
our fires a chief they have chosen! and without alu'kui.
   alu'kui?
   penis!
   excuse me mAri! you're very welcome, of course, kaci
   penelope, is not me, mAri, you shushuing! somebody appoint you
chief greeter?
                         and so many shades!
                         are you well?

we don't answer that question. except to say with what you could call arrogance, we are well. is so they leave you alone. i am marie lancet. ita?

why? oh! it just ain't safe for us.

i, ka'ci, have gathered into self, have waited her need since her sixth year.

is so? is mAri here. yuh doh by any chance know how many a-we it ha' in here? dey keep arrivin.

as there are poles in a house.

well, welcome, welcome. we use to have disagreement with She. is better if we so dont walk out too much in the day. i sorry to go so soon, but i've got to get back to the child. She know nothing 'bout caring for child, and besides that, is like She not here so much anymore.

i am the Caribbean
i ka'ci
                    my body my breath
          my sons too their fathers
        priests gods woven into you
          i bring with me the island
                    its songs and graces
the unbroken thread of all its knowing
    the breath before there was breath

        truly it is my time uati

so, ma ka'ci is why dat vine round yuh wris'?
rie girl! i ent see you so long! i thought you gone.
mAari, i here to stay, bes' fix to get on wit me, yes!
ka'ci you hungry? rie does make a great roti.
i ka'ci, would enjoy what is fish.

buh we ha fish, man. rie real expert wid fish curry.

ent is so, rie?

ka'ci is grateful.

i making four lil roti. She, ms lancet, ma ka'ci, an' me, we go eat. is na like de res a allyuh go starve.

penelope, your mind is bent on me.

ka'ci, you are a true carib?

as i have said.

forgive me, we were taught that you were uh um uh savage.

so said the foul ones with their evil spells. even wracked we refused them our world, or to travel the dawn land alone. many came with us to carry our shields. even as we left the body we fled to our streams, forest. they trembled then, knowing us in storm air. we filled their dreams with our blood. they know the acrid fear in the throat. they who are cannibal. who have scratched us down as they wish we were.

iropo'oti. their fear is fit. bu'meti. it is sweet.

pen-e-lope believe anyting anyting she read in buk. she nevah even tink who write de buk, o' how dey worl' think. or even wha kinda 'uman it take to go to somebody house, slaughter he, an take de house; far more, from who survive dey take dey worl', dey tongue, dey name, dey very self. worse dey tink dey got a right to take it. is wha dey gawdso teach dem . . .

mAri child why you get yourself so hot hot? Ka'ci just come out, get her a drink, cool yourself to think of something pleasant, be welcoming.

yes, ms lancet is right! you're so rude!

Ka'ci tell we her story, our story. yuh wan' preten' yuh ent here? yuh evah tink is pope nicolas wha start de whole thing? wha chain yuh drag yuh here? think 'bout de slaver-nun wha make saint in quebec. dese people dead worls. because dey wan' get rich! tink wha dat mean, penelope.

i'm thinking, i'm thinking! in this luxury flat!

wha she buy wid de pennyworth of all dey dun take off we back!

Lord help us!

wha Lawd? think! dey ent care wha dey do to dey own people. dey ent even care wha dey do to creashun. dey got nuclear weapon. now uranium tip missile to sicken de whole place!

mAri, you know every obscure fact to feed your bile. why can't you speak decent english?

an who say mi english ent decent? dem so wha say i born to be slave? it ha' anyting yuh unnerstan gurl?

ka'ci, is rie here, allyuh wan' argue or yuh wan' eat?

i kaci say to us all. time is greedy, will feed again as it has fed on us. but a clan that fights itself dies as a coward dies. yehe'meni-eti. it is evil. we cannot hold in such swirling bruising air. rie, this vine, its rich juice binds us into one.

we who are here stubborn
                    uninterruptable
ka'ima wa-ta'bura tune
let us draw water
            lakarahi'   gather
            ay-maeri   to eat
what matter the foreign weed once
choked the blue bell the black
ka'ima wa-ta'bura mam'ba
let us draw the honey
b'aca'rua get drunk
thou on peace ring out
thou on peace
            b'aca'rua

Penny Performs

dear jahmin

i have so heard of plain prose! of straight story!

Moral Masquerades

girl meets boy. girl seduces boy. girl gets pregnant. girl gives birth
to baby daughter. boy sues girl for making him a father without
his permission. demands custody of daughter. cites mother's
moral laxity: girl picked him up in bar. girl lied to him: "girls just
wanna have fun!" child ward of state. matter to supreme court,
the village elders of canadian society.

irony vanquished
left sarcasm's winter
summer's tantrum

that, sister, is called haiku

love

penny

Rie Performs

Lo mina

an' is wha appennin' wit you gurl
if yuh ent ha cocoa in de sun
is why yuh lookin fuh a rain
perhaps is phobia?
so wha we write sizzle yuh brain?
buh is why yuh ent like wonder ?
ent dese letta an' dem lead yuh
to de real heart a de palm
since duppy parasol is wha unfurl in drizzle
how come yuh fraid sheltah
buh chile is so much bettah to hol' chaati
ent wha is to is mus' is?

fuh me as fuh youso i tink nah is know i know   dem wha link
to earth an' trut' does dance so i run up jhandi
an' now yuh is to see we mina how
She search fuh we music
how She body de carpet hol' han'
out like net to ketch
melody where it float from star
from cloud trail from tree
like some kinda fairy moss
translucent how de bass come live
a earth pulse an' de patter
an' tempo a raindrops
is tenor pan

                    man is so we brush an' dip
        de slow suspirashun of a wave
                        or snowflake
        and de long easy body roll prairie put down
            how it startin' in heart pulse
                    how we muscle cheer it on
                    how afore conscious
                        t'ought surface we body
                            flow in a figure
                ben' to bass whirl to horn
        an' is how feet slip an' slide
    glide an' glance at de groun'
        how ankle turn an hol' while
            de body spin orf in dis space
                        music make an' She
                        spirit dress in meter
                do a barrel-leap turn saute an' twirl
    gurl dat tinglin' risin' from toes be de soul's own cheer
    is so we dances through dese room like Gawd's own
    prayer She self circlin tablas we settle in vital as blood
    infectious as joy when we swizzle we trini wine n wail
    we could heal sick translate dead gurl fren' She dance
    we a worl' from we motion tra-la-la-la-la mornin an'
    evenin tra-la-la-la-la brown gurl in de ring tra-la-la-la-
    la moon bloom in eyes out we mout' sapphire gurl
    show we yuh motion tra-la-la-la-la rainfores' from thigh
    allamanda from fingah is no wondah baby come

rie

PS is so Charlie cute   is a pity all his clothes an' dem pink.

Penelope Performs

jassy

already sometimes he sleeps all night and the days go so fast i
hardly realize how much we've done till i see folded piles of
washing so remember a square dim room cool whitewashed
thick tapia walls cracked oxblood floors sunlight in narrow
oblongs in half-door squares on a long raw-cedar kitchen table
a blanket folded at one end nearby on an upturned oil drum a
coal pot glows two flat irons bowl of rain water scent of hot
irons on sun bleached sun dried sheets clothes sprinkled damp
rolled into balls . . .

. . . jass, yuh ent fin' penelope real nostalgic? hear de voice. nobody tink
she talkin' slave labour. is wha all dat euro schoolin' do she. pen-e-lope ent
got no way to tink bout she own bein'. an' she so proud 'bout it! who
could 'magine dey pay some po' woman cents to stan' up fo' hours
scrubbin' at a wash-board? den stanin' ovah a hot coal pot ironin' fo'
even mo' hours. and is worse. she glad fo' de job. go from door to door
beggin' wuk. afterwards goin' in de cole cole mountain air. is so dem
woman end up wid dey flesh fall down ripplin' ovah dey boot . . .

the drops of lavender sprinkled light after

. . . steups! yuh cyan even wash yuh mout' on dis gurl is so she in she
glee with words. evryting evryting bright side fuh she cyan look de
worl' in de face!

above the gecko's constant tap tapping
shouts of men picking cashews the brothers'

shrill voices echo up the far slope's
camaraderie our bitter twisted fruit
                inside the house She
in She and i aside She the lone girlchild
        ran from kitchen to pantry
    from pantry to kitchen clumped up
                        grey concrete stairs
                    and down again
                underfoot noisy
in the quiet female voices near
            the ovens near the irons near the coal pots
                            underfoot we bounced through swing
doors
        wearing the dreadful silence around
    the stove the water barrels till
                    finally
        female
                underfoot and female
    "why don't you read that new book/do some needlework/do
                                    something?
            anyway you'd be better upstairs"
banished   empty rooms
                    alive   waiting some other
        voice we jumped on the beds
                    knocked things over
                screamed at the slightest hurt or scraped
        knee splinters
                and spears to the heart

She demanded succour
                    it was never enough
            days we lay curled
        the swaying squeaking hammock & we

108

with the avocado huge hard
by the back veranda
listened together for the falls' roar over plunging granite
v alley
e arth
r olling
t umbling
i rreparable
g arrulous
i nstinct
n udging
o ur
u ltimate
s urrender
to earth's voice its low
undecipherable story

but She was a butterfly searching
the forest's deep heart feeding
only from poinciana
angel's trumpet   (words
immortelles
yellow poui (phrases
her mouth climbing around them
seeking an entrance down which we could (
) but
deeper deeper safe dark deeper soft lit
for hours
safe dark we rode
over dreams
deeper we
rode our shadows
under grainy skies

```
         for days
             without secrets
    were safe and without   or our own
             epic strangeness              what
    days we surfaced  watched that which   is
             waited to catch               it
          something coming                 to be
       something that could explain        how
          we watched wondered              and
    wounded wonderwounded wondered   why
```

        an ocean swelling crashing in the head

the brothers stripped to the waist   their scrawny
bodies emerging from a cocoon of short trousers
already alight with certain importance   harvest the cashew
bright cloth tied around their heads keeping small sweat
from their eyes   they move tall   laugh with other men
i wait for them to stalk with my father
into the house   to bound stairs make proud
warrior noises   to splash in the tin
bath   to cough   roar at cold water   then call out
from behind half walls from under deepening
sky   its clear witness "what have you been
at all day long?" and She knows the great space
beside me where a sister should be . . .

. . . jahmin one night i asked "mother,
mother   how come you never
          had a sister for me?"

        her sudden face

                              my head slammed
                        hard back against the headboard
                              ringing

    rushing in my ears blood
    a flash flood on my tongue
    against my teeth   i
    to drink drinking
                                              i
    i
                i
                drunk   drank   i   shrunk
                ferocious silence
        pacing the dark   pale
        hemmed in with me
                                        five years i dreamt
                                            you jahmin yet
                            when you came a new terror rode me
                                    i didn't know   who
                    whether
gran said gently, "is a new baby, child, a new baby. is
    is all right" . . .
                    . . . giggle giggle gigglegiggle . . . a douen baby
a douen in a pen when the bough breaks the pe-enn will fall
            down will come Charlie pe-en and all . . . giggle
                gigglegigglegiggle . . .

. . . you see what's going on here, jasmine chile. is to pray.
pray . . .

. . . is na panic miz lancet. as long is on'y talk-so. we go
ha' sit up nite from now orn. one a we got to be alert all
all de time. ka'ci jes popup. mus' be strong fuh so. miz ka'ci?

tu-ki they make war tu-ki they make war
ka-ima kai wa-ku come my own come wake up
good! with her help we should be able to handle it. mAri,
ka'ci, if you could take first watch, ms lancet and i will do the rest.
pen-e-lope, we ha' to watch bot' nite an' day. wha allyou tink 'bout four
hours? dat way everbody ge' a li'l res'.
talking about body. we only have one between us. we'll have to walk
around quite a bit. stretch those muscles, pump those arms! it wouldn't
do to fall asleep.
Lord look down on us thy servants/stretch wide the wings
of the Holy Ghost/shelter us all and Charlie/in your divine grace/
alleluia the cross is with us/alleluia . . .

jassy, girl, most kids learn about babies by helping with sisters. She never
lifted you, never touched you, beyond a kiss light as sunbeam. only when
you were three She thirteen did She begin to lose her fear. you followed
us everywhere. now the bottles sparkling in a row the work is nothing.
what i will remember is playing with Charlie, milky sweet smell, feel of his
knees moving against my skin, hair like black curry of fisher clouds. mAri
and i will have to deal with the police when She disappears, at least so
we've planned. there's simply no other way. once She opens her mouth
we'll end up in wards full of truly crazy people. sis, how time collapses on
us. thanks for your offer of the beach house. till Charlie's papers are fixed,
i dream slow easy days under coconut palms. white sand in everywhere
including his mouth. crab callaloo, fresh fish. is there still free fish if you
help with the nets? phosphorescent night tides, laughing moons on swell
and curl of waves, stars?

do keep well. kiss the nephy. remind the husband he's no comedian.

love

penelope

JASMINE-MARIE LANCET MAINE

I DEMAND THAT YOU

EXCISE ME FROM THIS STORY

IMMEDIATELY

LEAVE ME OUT

PENELOPE-MARIE LANCET

Ms Lancet Performs

jasmine child

what going on here so sad sadder than lone child with bombed dead
She all listenin flutter restless searchin then nothin your sister sadder
than flies at iraqi eyes than soucouyant searchin for skin God know we
have to do somethin so i'm writin you   child   is slow slow it was goin
now before you call a name life hurtlin down the tracks   is all blur wild
rush flyin and i can't see! this gone too far jasmine . . .

                      . . . left us each other and night
             trapped in the one body in this conflict of memories
        and truths
                      barred the soul's reach for its own right
                            so barred from sight . . .

        . . . jahmin
dawn without rose day without shadow
             an even merciless light presents a world
        flattened to a mocking ordinariness that denies us small
pretensions or our necessary faith that we are makers of beauty
                      its spaciousness
        sweet as caimite
                            whose translucent white flesh
             star shaped gleaming black centre
                            is the grandmother's metaphor

                            . . . we whom las casas flared shorn
                      in the dank european storm . . .

. . . how this whole thing start. is to go back to when we only six years old.

. . . ya! true ignorance is bliss, bu' we born when She born. is only de waitin for She pain an need. mzzz lancet like tings neat an' linear. she like explanashun. make she feel like she in charge. in trut' she know bettah dan dat . . .

for nearly a year we was living quite in port of spain, in the capital to go to good school. living alone with an aunt. her hush-up house a thick scratchy blanket over the whole day. when we come home was like parole. so much noise and laugh and people. the mother and dad, the brothers, old auntie, miz pitsy in the kitchen with her tulum, and one weekend, a new nursemaid. hurt was we could only come home every other weekend. the brothers got to be home all all the time, climbing trees, playing red indian in the back yard, playing cricket, bomber pilot, soccer, going to school with Dad. then, one weekend we come home. it have a tiny baby. Thena-Marie was a real surprise. everybody busy busy fussing, too busy to take much notice of we. is then we understand why they send us away. i think first we start by wanting to be baby. but is clear that ain't have no future. then we figure if we good as gold, help with baby, fuss over it, Mother and Dad would notice probably love us again. you know for a while it really work. pretty soon Mother praising we to the skies. Dad calling we "his big girl" boasting how good we is with little sister. every other weekend.

is a sad thing but people just don't take children serious. nowhere, nowhere. right here where it full of psychology, just watch how they does talk, how they does treat children. like child ain't got no complexity. i always wonder if things different in the old africa.

one easter holiday the whole family was up at lopinot, and She was holding the baby, standing near She brothers looking into the well. the men preparing to clean it. by then baby Thena was one year old or so and we was nearly eight. one minute everything going on fine, the next minute Thena leap.

is to hear a kind of ohh! . . .

. . . jahmin

jahmin

my arms full of nothing. then a scream, Thena's thin cry. i lean over, gone from myself, my body filling up with the cold, gleaming dark of well water. and then a kind of thud. then another. a loud silence echoing. a long while after, a splash. chipped concrete of well rim cutting cold against. somebody holding me by the waist and pulling. a various crying out and shouting. people catching rope, somebody calling God God oh God! a murmuring falling into silence. we are pushed back, and pulled into light. the brothers staring wide eyed at me. a harsh voice give orders, then ramsley, what used to take us to roam the coffee, sliding down, down. at the last he looks up. his flared nostrils, his sun-reddened eyes, their glimmer. he sink as if into his own rippling darkness.

the world under glass
                        distinct the brother breathing
through his mouth   the ragged field
breathes with him
                        sunlight merciless bouncing off leaves
off the new domed tin cover off the sweaty bulging arms
   of workers clustered   staring
the rim
         the deep
    their competent scarred hands circle rest on
idle ropes   lean on brooms   rakes   cutlasses
                              grasped hard

miz bodin leading the charge of neighbours
                        miss olive on the slope
hand to her mouth
                  her grey apron bellies in the wind

                         i at insufficient air

and Mother come hurrying to the well
                        not crying out not
running silent blind to everything

                              she waits like a cloud heavy
trailing rain
a piling up of thunder

she never looks at me

then ramsley called out from the well, his voice echoing round the walls
"bucket." i didn't know what he meant. i thought he'd say "found her"
any/something like that. i leant to look as it came up, clanking once
against stone. the man hauling on the rope, "sorry!" quick glance at my
mother. somebody grabbed me, pulling me back again, before i could
really see . . .

                              and Mother lifts Thena
and the clear amber smell of well water into her arms. she buries buries
her face her face in Thena.

Thena drip drips overflowing. like it have more dread than she one so small
could hold. then Mother turns away, walks heavy up the slope to the house.
blood running watery stains her dress at the shoulder.
                                      i was holding tight
        not my fault
                              he got her out
                i didn't mean it   Thena
        i couldn't help it
                                      Dad angry
                angry   yell yell yell
                              i must it was an accident!
        run
                run away
                              he'll find me yell yell
        she jumped   i couldn't
                        Thena's always getting me into trouble
                                      i'll hide
                i'll run away
        my fault

                    she jumped jumped she jumped
        Thena i couldn't hold on

. . . sigh coughcough sighsigh oh oh . . . she took her by
                her left leg an' threw her down the stairs
        goosey goosey gander . . . giggglegiggle giggle where
                shall you wander wander wander giggle giggglegiggle
giggle . . .

        Thena she's always jumping

    they'll kill me
                        i didn't mean it
        Thena Thena still
                            sleeping

i and the brothers walk behind her in a file with two of the men. even
then, i, already separate from the brothers, already in different worlds.
at the house i sit small on a pouf near the back wall, melt into the
dimmest corner of the living room. for a long time nothing. then doctor
comes and goes, glancing at us. county nurse with Mother and Thena
behind the closed door. Dad comes back from work. Mother holding his
face in both hands shakes her head. tears on her cheeks. they go straight
into their room and shut the door. no greeting. his eyes look at me as
if i'm not there. he even forgets to hug the brothers.

        the house hushes itself

            no raps no clinks no murmurs rising

            no passersby call out greetings

        i cannot hear my brothers breathing

    time does not pass

                or rather passes silently

i cannot tell

time

or hear past this still air

even the gecko who lives in the ceiling deserts

i try not to think of blood   my breathing slows

slows

i think i must say sorry. i must find out how Thena is. if they're going to hit me i want to get it over with. i wait for a long long time on my pouf. the brothers go out to the back verandah. mz bodin comes in with a covered tray goes down stairs. nobody comes. nennen arrives, goes into the room. i wait. aunt lucy. neighbours sit awhile whispering in patois. i wait. after a long long while i pick up courage in both hands, knock on the door.

Dad opens it. no smile.

i say in a rush, but stumbling a little over her name and the fear-clutch in the gut, "is Th — Thena . . . is Thena getting better?"

look like a blow. like a cuff in the mouth.

"O God, Penelope, you ain't see? Your sister is dead! Thena dead! You understand? I don't want you bothering your mother. In a little while your grandmother is going to be here. Go tidy up. What you have to say?"

the breath gone from my vocal cords. heart-squeezed.

i stared.

"I can't hear you!"

"iisssorry . . . iiisosssorrysssorryissor . . ."

"Now stop bothering your mother!"

"i sor . . . sorry . . . sorrii . . ."

the door closes hard.

sssorrysorry . . .

how dead? Thena is a baby. dead? i imagine a great terrifying darkness. Thena alone in it. dead. my mind fills with horror. silence sniffing at my ankles, pawing my yellow shorts, circling. i am shut into a vast hollow space. shrinking. in our room, sheila, Thena's nursemaid, crying, glares at me, packing her things to go home. i hear a horn. a truck with a tin coffin and blocks of ice. a man and a boy. she will be cold. the boy forgets the lid. he is sent back to get it. dark. she'll hate it. dark. shut in. she won't be able to breathe! i am frantic to tell them not to put the lid on. dead. i sit shivering on my bed. Thena's empty crib. i curl up shivering. a hand on my back, patting. gran's voice a whisper, "an accident, baby, an accident." she draws a blanket over me. i am not a baby. i am a big sister. Thena is a baby. gran pats. i fall asleep. when i wake up. it's dark. Thena not in her crib. still dead.

that evening grandmothers, aunts and uncles shushuing shushuing. i killed Thena. cousins, godmothers shushuing. visitors come to sit with family. i have to sit too, swinging my foot in its royal blue chinese slipper. pale flowers in tiny perfect stitches that look padded. near the big toe one yellow flower unravelling. shushuing and staring. or not staring. i swing my foot and swing. dead. nen says suddenly, "an accident. could happen to anybody." her voice harsh. i hide under the stairs. a brother comes to get me. he looks sorry for me. nobody, not Mother not Dad, wants to say anything to me. nobody wants to touch us. see us. not a word beyond "good night," "finish your supper, please," "go to bed." nobody hit me. nobody kissed me good night.

friday. "good morning, slept well?" vexed-with-you voice. Thena not sleeping. she is dead. forever. "wear your white blouse and the black skirt." "clean your shoes." "find something to do." dead. i walk down to the well. struggle to lift the cover off. "buh look at dat chile? leff dat be!" "get away from dere." "buh eh eh!" "is wha wrong wit' she?" the workers. i run back inside. afraid. gran says quietly, "penny, don't go out there. go in your room, child, and read something." dead. i couldn't figure it out. at seven o'clock that night, the whole village gathers in our house for prayers. we pray near the brothers, wanting a miracle, promising to be good forever and ever.

saturday. "don't you be playing outside the house." i wasn't. i was just standing on the front verandah. "go inside." "read a book." "nan will comb your hair." "you have a handkerchief?" a new stiff white organdy dress with black polka dots. black ribbons. all scratchy. a hearse, black cars. the country church. Thena looking as if she is sleeping. my lips brush an icy cheek. at the grave side we hear earth and stones thunking on tiny tiny white coffin. and dream about it and dream about it and dream about it and dream.

afterwards, in the newspapers. the brothers show me my name. naked. staked to a page. the whole world staring. next sunday at confession the irish priest asks, "did you love your sister?" yes. "did you let her fall deliberately?" silence. "how did it really happen?" silence. i shake my head. i can't remember. not exactly. "are you sure?" Thena'd gone straight to heaven. if i hadn't done it deliberately, i had nothing to worry about. "Thena-Marie is a holy innocent."

jasmine child, afterwards every policeman is terror. we don't know how long it take before they come for you. before they hang you. one day a brother say "policeman asking for you." brap! is drop the teapot to our doll set, run to look out the window to see if it really have a tall man in grey and blue uniform. it have. She run an' hide in a shed in the back-yard, behind the fowl run. She know then we kill Thena. otherwise he wouldn't be there. we hear the shouting and calling our name.

once a man came into the shed. we stop breathing there in the dark under a pile of feed sacks. he went away. next morning, coming to feed the chickens they found us. She had a fever. doctor samuels came. we had fits. the priest came. extreme unction. uncle doctor came. Dad holding her, rocking her all night. She began to get better. poco a poco.

after that they say She always talking to Sheself. "child, what wrong with you? keep on talking to yourself so, and they going take you to the madhouse in st anne's, you know." and they took us to uncle doctor again. questions. "i can't remember." "i can't remember." one night, months later, a thief tried to get into the house in town where She still went to school with aunt. a dry skinny brown leg, pant rolled up above the ankle, long narrow bare brown foot, toes groping. shivering, sleepless, shrivelling. he wasn't a thief. he'd come to get us. he knew where She lived. poor aunt getting desperate.

Dad decided we and aunt should come back home to live. we had was to take that long tiring train to town school every day. everybody, everybody, even teachers, niceing up. one day a girl call we killer. somebody run and tell, then teacher take out she strap. after that, is no damn dog bark!

jasmine child, long before She recover from the illness, went back to school, your parents give 'way all Thena's things. hide all the photographs. was good. She forget. everybody think was for the best. they say we talk in our sleep. we make a rule. mAri and i only come out at night. after awhile, penelope join She in school. and we make a pact. if She coming out during the day is best She forget all about Thena. besides mAri didn't like school. i ain't fraid of no douen, and penny fraid she own shadow.

well, jasmine child, i hope you satisfy with this. though it must be a shock. i don't think you knew about Thena. Charlie doing okay, he have the neatest little smile. they have stuff in the papers and so, but not to worry. we do take care of She. i'm glad that after all that work, hurricane stephen pass you by. allyou real lucky. and is how C L R doing? you ain't say a thing about him in your letter. except for mAri going out every night to africadey, things going fine. Charlie's in the study, so nobody to hear him screamin'. is not how anybody could want things, but mAri strong for so. is nobody to stop her doing what she want, and She ain't able.

love

marie lancet

Penny Performs

jahmin

look where the cowled moon
hurries home dark alleys lined
with nod
                                                        his winking

                blinking
brothers

i too walk the shadows
where vines rattle rotting walls
and purple moss campion
blows brave

sister i am no longer brave
who walks with me?

love

penny

mAri Performs

(wit intruptions . . .)

jass

buh gurl is so long nobody ent hear from yuh cyan be Cyril
wha keepin yuh so busy busy! jass here we drownin in trouble
fuh once ms lancet right! things ent goin good . . .

                    . . . the last sunrays unfazed
(this wind this sudden rain
                    diss shadows gathered on the bluff . . .

jahmin
                    i drift before blank pages
                    before the unremembered unlived . . .

. . . everybody everybody ha somethin' to say an' nobody ha de
strengt' to create order   yuh see fo' yuhself how ah cyan . . .
. . . these little deaths   jahmin are all that's left . . .
. . . an' piece of She is all we got . . .
        as i sayin fore i get interrupt, jass, yuh tink yuh wan truth

                de woeman move
                        to where de great hall
            of noon hesitate
                in shadow an' She too
                    hesitate
                            a laggard star
slow
                    watery

                              yet   deliberate
She bare foot claim
        de place She step
            dis ent no . . .
    . . . beauty full in her walk
            She move in de common way
                a woeman
            takin accounta gravity
            takin account
                        wid out t'ought
                is so She come to dis place wey
                    de mirror eyein her
                slide wide-open   de Widow Thought
            She   to stan' up in dat glare
        a bird bleed from nothin
                a bird fallin to python
                            She freeze

            . . . don't read don't! sister listen where
        a wheel its spokes speak her from head to heel . . .

    . . . narcissus in straw boater
                and red turtle kneeling
            beside a slough
                        to gesture her image
            into minute being
                            among weeds
        in dark drift   in dapple
            "i would hide in soft
                converse with me only me . . ."
    . . . She siddown dere on stool i put to save She from long standin' . . .

. . . now consider her
alert, jassy
to the mirror's possibility
its greedy snap   her
unsurrendered
flesh its swallow
her form
its dark-for-so-ness
all wavering
as in water . . .

. . . jahmin . . .

. . . She dun stop takin pill an' dem, jest sittin dere. readin
as usual She don't hear de chile. de res a-we fine but . . .
. . . listen how that other rattles along! . . .

. . . jahmin how can i tell you of me my face
the mirror's depths my face always on the verges

swirling
how other
eyes
smiles
ripple out
ech-echoes
echoing
ecce
ecce

fading
i

i fey

faint

. . . rie here, mina, yuh bettah get here do something . . .
. . . its crazed colours mock
our dim dailiness . . .

. . . we faces swimmin up
nah is bettah to say
eyes huge oval glimm . . .

. . . gurl dey done pick-up some po' woeman an charge she wit' stealin
baby. yuh know is probably de woeman own chile. de people wha' dopt
our Charlie from God know who say dey so glad to ha he back! DNA is a
blessin . . .

. . . jassy She stares into the mirror
as one from the rocky coves
at blanchiseusse
hurricaned into welter
might gaze out at the atlantic
searching for survivors
just so she seeks in her reflection
other vague irregular faces
as if with grave
exhausted strokes they
might rise from unfathomed
depths to greet her

. . . mina gurl, we healthier dan She buh dis body dead weary a sittin in fronta computer . . .

jass yuh know is so penelope impatient eh! she tire a' dat an' take over buh was fifteen twenty minutes She stan' up dere staring at dat mirror   She coulda turn hibiscus . . .

she means narcissus of course . . .

nutten a de sort! ah mean, jass, yuh wan' real action?
dat's it.

in any case, jassy, She is your sister, remember only the something inherited spread like a thin gauze through her . . .

she mean all-a allyuhso . . .

these things are probably in the genes, you've read your *Bell Curve* . . .

which is proof of his genes, if nutten else. jass, if pen-e-lope so wan' to write, i leavin' it to her. kiss C.L.R. for mi, an' say hello to yuh man. is gorn ah gorn.

PS   is why yuh don' write pen-e-lope a letter explain she how racism start in the eighteenth century?   yuh know how she is. she ent want read 'bout slave even if is a white man wha write de book

. . . my face
            changing face
        a mask in the forest
                think of the naked bear
the hairless one who greets
"i am the one who eats you."

. . . by the way did She tell you of the time we took Charlie to sears? girl, She start up the escalator and as soon as She step off Charlie start to scream. well, you know how penelope is, she want the baby to behave. she don't want people staring. so penelope pop up and get right back on the escalator, and travel back down to the main floor and start for the door, head in de air, neck like a giraffe. rie ain't care about nothing an' you know how she mousy lookin', she pop up, start back and up the escalator, neck sink down like turtle, face like mule. girl, i just stay quiet and watch. rie riding up, penelope riding down. is clear something gone wrong. plus rie like to take quick peeks at sheself in all those mirrors. after about ten minutes of this people gathering, some of them pretending to shop, but they staring. the one or two clerks they have, top floor bottom floor, now watching openly. rie hit baby's clothes section, step off, Charlie start up. penelope pop up, the head gone up in the air, the neck stretch, she face get this supercilious look, like she don't know she have this baby screaming in her arms, and start down again. Charlie just enjoying the ride.

finally a man come up and ask what she doing. he say she can't ride the escalator is not a carnival. penelope in she hunt-bellow english accent, "My dear man, I am obviously calming the baby. Rie doesn't care whether he's disturbing your clients. I do. (Charlie know he not moving start to howl.) Satisfied are you? Are you? Am I disturbing other shoppers? Hogging the escalator?" she sniff rie? who is rie? the poor guy look like he get punch. she step right back on the escalator and gone back up. now she on the high horse. she ride up, she ride down. rie pop up, see how people staring. is now she just want to get out of the store.

but penelope in charge. down once, twice, three times. then she consent to let rie buy the child a couple of cute little suits and a pair of denim rompers. worse, all the way home the poor taxi driver eyes bulging while the two of them switching back and forth. both of them furious so poor charlie getting squeeze an' tension high. he start to scream. two voices, you could say two persons. but it only have one woman in the cab, the man drive like he crazy, drive like a madman. take the hill like is a jump, an the cab is a horse. one good thing. he didn't even wait for his fare. since money real tight . . .

. . . even riding escalators at Sears
my faces my voice refusing silence appear and disappear
my lonely lovely selves call in the Bow sky's wide silence
insisting

the woman in dim blue and inward eye the man looking around searching for a face the girl in classic hair clutching at shopping bags past women's clothing past children's past the newest vulgar designs for stucco houses past giggling teenagers running down the years all all of us looking for something looking to something to do for us what

this simple breathing in and out has not what love has not nor prayers
nor what we've been taught we ought . . .

. . . miz lancet a knock at de door . . .

                              . . . we
to memory as a toddler a wild rocking horse . . .

. . . cough coughsigh mummy's got a bunting rock and rock
an giggle giggle gigglegigglegiggle ALL FALL DOWN
                    giggle giggle ALL FALL DOWN . . . giggle giggle . . .

. . . Lord is marie lancet i asking you AGAIN to come to our aid . . .

now miz lancet takin' orn Gawd! allyuh crazy, yes!
        rie, yuh here too! wha yuh mean "allyuh"?
        mArie, i can still hear some one knocking. i thought you
and miz lancet . . .
        . . . jasmine

                    KNOCKknockKNOCK

        you remember the lapwing child
                and its persistent noble stance
                        in the pasture near caroni there
            that fire-breathed dry season of the bees?
            how its trance of pain
                    its frantic flap an' brush against
                        such heavy stalks
            how its flutterin broken winged dance

is so it is with your sister . . .

BANGknockknockknockBANG   BANG   BANG

. . . miz lancet ent somebody knockin' de door? o Lawd! miz lancet, yuh
respectable, go see . . .

        . . . jahmin
                        last night
                whistle of a ghost train past
                        an abandoned well

                weeping its dark water
                        a sickle moon

. . . o Gawd miz lancet! buh . . .
        allyuhso ent hear de poundin' somebody turn' key in lock.
        rie, we got to hide is de police . . .
        everybody calm down. i'm going to open the door. nobody talks
except me! do you hear the chain? shut . . . butterfly . . .
up! . . . moments
                        heliconi moments haunted
                        by else
                        and languor . . .

(more pounding
sound of chain being rattled)

        "Penny! PENNY!"
        "Okay okay I'M COMMING! I was sleeping. Must have BEEN DREAMING!
dreaming actually. just a minute justaminutejust . . ."

(pounding   sharp slam   door busted open   footsteps
                        caretaker and a woman)

                "One hell of a dream!"
                "Oh! Oh . . . um . . . Miss Lancet?"

Jassy!
"Penny! Penny, you're sitting here typing!   Where's Charla?"
o Gawd gurl you well frighten we! Charlie in de bedroom
well, jasmine chile, i can't tell you is how i please to see you.
ent penelope tell allyuh is to shut up!

"Penny! Penny!"

. . . giggle   gigglegiggle   gigglegigglegiggle . . . mummy's going
to buy you a MOCKING BIRD . . . giggle giggle giggle . . . and if that
mocking bird don't sing . . . giggle . . . mummy's going to buy you
a diamond ring and if that diamond ring be brass, mummy's . . . giggle
gigglegigglegiggle . . . mummy's going . . . gigglegiggle to buy you
a looking glass giggle gigglegiggle . . .

. . . pen-ny pen-ny . . .

"Oh my God!   Penny!"

. . . penny?
pen-ny . . .